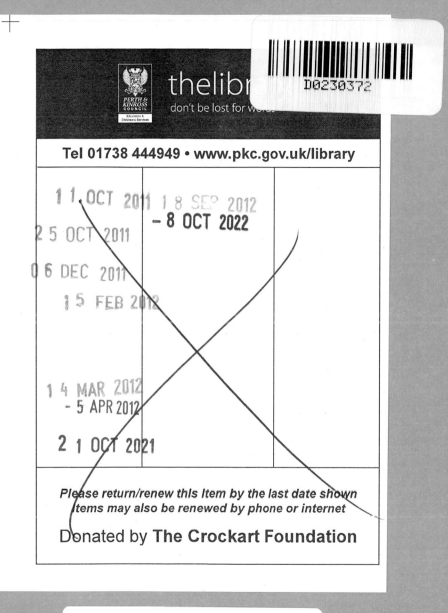

Annabel Karmel
Top 100 Meals in Minutes

Annabel Karmel
Top 100 Meals in Minutes

Quick and easy meals for babies and toddlers

EBURY
PRESS

To Nicholas, Lara and Scarlett

10 9 8 7 6 5 4 3 2 1

Published in 2011 by Ebury Press, an imprint of Ebury Publishing

Ebury Publishing is a division of the Random House Group

Text © Annabel Karmel 2011
Photography © Dave King 2011

Annabel Karmel has asserted her right to be identified as the author of
this Work in accordance with the Copyright, Designs and Patents Act 1988

The Random House Group Limited Reg. No. 954009

Addresses for companies within the Random House Group can be found
at www.randomhouse.co.uk

A CIP catalogue record for this book is available from the British Library

The Random House Group Limited supports the Forest Stewardship
Council® (FSC®), the leading international forest certification organisation.
All our titles that are printed on Greenpeace approved FSC® certified
paper carry the FSC® logo. Our paper procurement policy can be found at
www.randomhouse.co.uk/environment.

Printed and bound in China by C&C Offset Printing Co, Ltd.

Design & illustrations: Smith & Gilmour Ltd, London
Photography: Dave King
Food stylist: Seiko Hatfield
Props stylist: Jo Harris
Shoot stylist: Liz Beckett
Copy editor: Jo Godfrey Wood

ISBN 978-0-09-193900-7

CONTENTS

Easy peasy pureés and finger foods

Easy peasy purées

There are many purées that don't need any cooking at all. All of these fruit and vegetable purées can be prepared in minutes.

Peach purée 15

Sweet ripe peaches are delicious and easy to digest. Stir in some baby rice if the purée is too runny.

1 large, ripe juicy peach
A little baby rice (optional)

◉ Score a cross with a sharp knife on the base of the peach. Place it in a small bowl and pour boiling water over it.

◉ Drain, then rinse in cold water; the skin should then peel away easily. Cut the flesh away from the stone and mash or purée.

◉ You may want to stir in a little baby rice as it will probably be very runny.

Peach and banana  15

1 ripe juicy peach
½ small ripe banana

◉ Skin the peach (as above) and cut the flesh away from the stone. Mash it together with the banana using a fork or you could use a hand blender.

◉ Serve on its own or mixed with a little baby rice.

Mango purée

5

Known as the 'King of Fruit', mangoes are an antioxidant – a rich health booster.

½ medium ripe mango

◉ Remove the skin from the halved mango and cut the flesh into cubes.

◉ Mash or purée in a food processor until smooth.

Mango and banana

5

½ small, ripe mango
½ small, ripe banana

◉ Prepare the mango as for the mango purée.

◉ Slice the banana.

◉ Mash the banana and mango or purée in a hand blender.

Mango and strawberry

5

½ small ripe mango
2 strawberries, hulled

◉ Prepare the mango as in the mango purée.

◉ Blend the mango flesh together with the strawberries.

Apple, strawberry and banana purée

15

Strawberries are rich in vitamin C and have a natural sweetness which makes this delicious.

SUITABLE FOR FREEZING
SUITABLE FROM 6 MONTHS
MAKES 3 PORTIONS
2 sweet eating apples, peeled and chopped (approx 175g/6 oz peeled weight)
60 g (2½ oz) strawberries, hulled and quartered
½ small banana

◉ Put all the ingredients in a saucepan and cook over low heat for about 8 minutes, or until the apples are tender then purée with an electric hand blender.

Pear, apple and blueberry purée

15

Blueberries contain more antioxidants than any other fruits.

SUITABLE FOR FREEZING
SUITABLE FROM 6 MONTHS
MAKES 3 PORTIONS
2 ripe pears, peeled
2 dessert apples, peeled
100 g (3½ oz) blueberries
2–3 tbsp water

◉ Remove the core from the pear and apples. Roughly chop them and place in a saucepan with the water and blueberries.

◉ Simmer for 8–10 minutes, until soft. Whiz until smooth, using a hand blender.

Plum 10

Always make sure that you taste the fruit before giving it to your baby – some plums can be quite sour but sweet ones are delicious.

SUITABLE FOR FREEZING
SUITABLE FROM 6 MONTHS
MAKES 1 PORTION
2 large plums
baby rice, crumbled rusk, mashed banana (optional)

◉ Skin 2 large plums in the same way as you skin a peach (see page 8). Chop the flesh.

◉ Purée the plums uncooked if ripe and juicy, or steam them for a few minutes until tender. They are good mixed with baby rice, crumbled rusk or mashed banana.

Peach and blueberry 15

You could use nectarines instead of peaches. Sweet white nectarines are especially good.

SUITABLE FOR FREEZING
SUITABLE FROM 6 MONTHS
MAKES 2 PORTIONS
2 medium, ripe peaches
40 g (1½ oz) blueberries

◉ Skin the peaches and cut into chunks.

◉ Put into a saucepan with the blueberries and cook for 3 minutes over medium heat.

◉ Blend to a purée.

Banana ● 5

Banana makes perfect portable baby food as it comes in its own packaging. Banana is good for the treatment of both diarrhoea and constipation.

NOT SUITABLE FOR FREEZING
SUITABLE FROM 6 MONTHS
MAKES 1 PORTION
Half a small banana
A little breast or formula milk (optional)

◉ Simply mash the banana with a fork. During the first stages of weaning add a little of your baby's usual milk, if necessary, to thin down the consistency and provide a familiar taste.

Papaya ● 5

Papaya is rich in vitamin C and beta-carotene. Papaya is also high in soluble fibre, which is important for normal bowel function.

NOT SUITABLE FOR FREEZING
SUITABLE FROM 6 MONTHS
MAKES 1 PORTION
Half a small ripe papaya

◉ Cut the papaya in half, remove the black seeds, scoop out the flesh and mash or purée until smooth.

Avocado ⏾ 5

Avocados contain more nutrients than any other fruit. They are rich in vitamin E, which also boosts the immune system. They are also rich in monounsaturated fat, the good type of fat. Babies need nutrient dense foods and the high-calorie content of avocados makes them an ideal food for growing babies.

NOT SUITABLE FOR FREEZING
SUITABLE FROM 6 MONTHS

MAKES 1 PORTION
Half small ripe avocado
A little breast or formula milk (optional)

◉ Simply cut the avocado in half and remove the stone. Scoop out the flesh and mash together with a little of your baby's usual milk.

Avocado and banana ⏾ 5

This is a popular combination.

NOT SUITABLE FOR FREEZING
SUITABLE FROM 6 MONTHS
MAKES 1 PORTION
1/2 small avocado
1/2 small ripe banana, peeled
1 to 2 tbsp of your baby's usual milk

◉ Mash the avocado and banana together and, if you like, stir in a little of your baby's usual milk.

Sweet potato, carrot and sweetcorn

Some vegetables, such as sweet potato, carrot, butternut squash, pumpkin and sweetcorn are naturally sweet and these are popular with babies. Orange-coloured root vegetables are also rich in betacarotene, which is essential for growth, healthy skin and fighting infection.

1 small sweet potato (225g/8 oz), peeled and chopped
1 medium carrot approximately 75g (3 oz), peeled and chopped
2 tbsp cooked fresh, frozen corn or canned corn

◉ Put the sweet potato and carrot into a steamer and cook for about 15 minutes, or until tender.

◉ Purée together with the corn and 4 tablespoons of the water from the bottom of the steamer.

Lovely lentil purée

You might not have thought of giving your baby lentils, but some of my most popular baby recipes are lentil purées. Lentils are a good source of protein, iron and fibre. They are good for all babies and especially good to include in your baby's diet if you are a vegetarian.

1 tbsp sunflower oil
50 g (2 oz) onion, finely chopped
2 medium carrots, chopped
   (100g/3½ oz)
2 tbsp celery, chopped
50 g (2 oz) split red lentils, rinsed
1 medium (225g/8 oz) sweet potato, peeled and chopped
300 ml (½ pint) unsalted vegetable stock or water
30g (1 oz) Cheddar cheese, grated

◉ Sauté the onion, carrot and celery in the oil for about 5 minutes, or until softened.

◉ Add the lentils and sauté for one minute. Stir in the sweet potato and pour over the stock or water.

◉ Bring to the boil, turn down the heat and simmer covered for about 20 minutes or until the lentils are soft.

◉ Purée in a blender and stir in the grated cheese until melted.

Lentil and vegetable purée

A tasty purée with nutritious ingredients and I have sped up the cooking process by using lentils in a tin. Lentils are a good non-meat source of iron. One of the reasons why it is important to introduce solids at six months is because the iron a baby inherits from his or her mother runs out at this age – so it is important to introduce iron-rich foods.

1 tbsp olive oil
50 g (2 oz) leek, finely chopped
50 g (2 oz) carrot, finely chopped
½ clove garlic, crushed
50 g (2 oz) cooked green lentils
   from a tin, drained and rinsed
200 g (7 oz) tin chopped tomatoes
100 ml (3½ fl oz) water
1 tsp tomato purée
1 small bay leaf
1 ready to eat apricot, chopped
1 tbsp fresh basil
2 tbsp natural yogurt (not low fat)

◉ Heat the oil in a saucepan. Add the leek, carrot and garlic. Sauté for 5 minutes.

◉ Add the lentils, tomatoes, water, tomato purée, bay leaf and apricot. Bring to the boil. Cover and simmer for 8 to 10 minutes.

◉ Whiz using a hand blender until smooth. Stir in the basil and yoghurt.

Mashed sweet potato with spinach

A good way to introduce stronger-tasting green vegetables is to mix them together with sweet tasting root vegetables. Low fat dairy products are not suitable for young children as they need the calories to fuel their rapid growth.

150 g (5½ oz) peeled and
    chopped sweet potato
125 g (4½ oz) peeled and
    chopped potato
200 ml (7 fl oz) boiling water
40 g (1½ oz) fresh baby spinach
30 g (1 oz) frozen peas
40 g (1½ oz) Cheddar, grated
1 tbsp milk

◉ Put the sweet potato and potato into a pan, cover with boiling water and cook, covered, for 10 minutes.

◉ Add the spinach and peas, cover and cook for 3 minutes. Uncover and, if any liquid is still left, cook a little longer.

◉ Stir in the grated cheese and milk, then whiz until smooth, using a hand blender.

Pasta shells with butternut squash and tomato sauce

This fresh tomato sauce is very tasty and because it has butternut squash and cheese blended into it, it is more nutritious than an ordinary tomato sauce.

150 g (5½ oz) butternut squash, peeled and chopped
2 tbsp mini shell pasta
3 medium tomatoes
15 g (½ oz) butter
30 g (1 oz) Cheddar cheese, grated

◉ Steam the butternut squash for 10 minutes, or until tender.

◉ Cook the pasta according to the packet instructions. Meanwhile, skin the tomatoes, as in the next step.

◉ Cut a cross in the base of the tomatoes using a sharp knife. Put them in a bowl and cover with boiling water. Leave for one minute. Drain and rinse in cold water. The skin should peel off easily. Cut the tomatoes into quarters and deseed.

◉ Melt the butter in a small saucepan and sauté until mushy. Stir in the cheese until melted.

◉ Blend the butternut squash with the tomato and cheese sauce. Drain the pasta and stir into the sauce.

Poached salmon with sweet potato and peas

It's hard to find a jar of baby purée that contains oily fish such as salmon, yet the essential fatty acids in oily fish are particularly important for the development of your baby's brain or nervous system and vision. Fats like these are a major component of the brain – for this reason 50 per cent of the calories in breast milk are composed of fat.

150 ml (¼ pint) vegetable stock or water

125 g (4½ oz) sweet potato, peeled and chopped

100 g (3½ oz) salmon fillet, skinned, cut into 1 cm (3/8 in) cubes

2 tbsp frozen peas

40 g (1½ oz) mature Cheddar cheese, grated

◉ Put the stock or water in a saucepan with the sweet potato. Bring to the boil, then cook over a medium heat for 7–8 minutes, or until the sweet potato is just tender.

◉ Add the salmon and peas, cover again and simmer for 3–4 minutes, until the fish flakes easily and the vegetables are tender.

◉ Remove from the heat and stir in the grated cheese. Blend to a purée for young babies or mash for older babies.

◉ Cool as quickly as possible, then cover and chill. You can freeze it in individual portions, thaw overnight in the fridge, then reheat until piping hot. Stir and allow to cook slightly before serving.

Cod with sweet potato

If you want your baby to enjoy eating fish, then introduce it early. You can give them fish from 6 months. Begin with mildly flavoured white fish such as cod or Pollock, with a favourite vegetable purée or a cheese sauce.

knob of butter
100 g (3½ oz) onion, finely chopped
150 g (3½ oz) peeled, sweet potato, roughly chopped
150 ml (1/4 pint) milk
1 small bay leaf
100 g (3½ oz) cod fillet, skinned and sliced into 4 cm (2 inch) pieces

◉ Melt the butter in a saucepan. Add the onion and sauté for 5 minutes, until nearly soft.

◉ Add the potatoes, milk and bay leaf. Bring up to the boil, cover and simmer for 10 minutes, until the potatoes are tender.

◉ Add the cod and cook for another 2 to 3 minutes. Remove the bay leaf, then whiz using a hand blender to make a fine purée. You can mash for older babies.

Cherub's chowder

Fats from dairy produce, such as butter, cheese, yoghurt and milk are fine for babies and they provide vitamins A and D. It is not good just to give them fruit and vegetable purées, since they are low in calories.

knob of butter
1 small celery stick, finely diced
1 small leek, roughly chopped
1 small carrot, peeled and finely diced
100 g (3½ oz) potatoes, peeled and chopped into small dice
1 tbsp plain flour
350 ml (11 fl oz) milk
15 g (½ oz) Parmesan cheese, grated
½ tsp Dijon mustard
150 g (3½ oz) cod or haddock, skinned and sliced into 2 cm (¾ in) cubes
1 tbsp chives, chopped
½ tsp lemon juice

◉ Melt the butter in a saucepan. Add the celery, leek, carrot and potatoes. Coat in the butter and gently sauté for 3–4 minutes. Sprinkle over the flour.

◉ Add the milk, stir until blended. Bring up to the boil, stirring until thickened. Cover and simmer for 8 minutes, until the vegetables are cooked.

◉ Add the cheese, Dijon mustard and haddock and continue to simmer for 5 minutes, until the haddock is cooked through. Stir in the chives and lemon juice.

Baby's first fish pie

Although you should continue with formula or breast milk for the whole of the first year, full-fat cow's milk can be used in cooking and with cereals from 6 months.

SUITABLE FOR FREEZING
SUITABLE FROM 6 MONTHS
MAKES 4 PORTIONS

200 g (7 oz) peeled potatoes, diced
1 small onion, finely diced
100 ml (3½ fl oz) milk
100 ml (3½ fl oz) weak fish stock
50 g (2 oz) frozen peas
150 g (3½ oz) cod, skinned and sliced into small cubes
1 tsp lemon juice
3 tbsp Parmesan cheese, grated
1 tsp dill, chopped

◉ Put the potatoes and onion into a saucepan. Cover with the milk and weak fish stock. Bring to the boil, cover and simmer for 10 minutes.

◉ Add the peas and cod and continue to cook for 5 minutes.

◉ Whiz to a purée in a blender. Add the lemon juice, cheese and dill.

Salmon smash 35

As your baby gets older you can mash rather than purée the food. This is a delicious combination of mashed potato, carrot and broccoli with flaked salmon. The healthy fats found in oily fish encourage growth as well as the development of your baby's brain, nervous system and vision.

SUITABLE FOR FREEZING
SUITABLE FROM 7 MONTHS
MAKES 3 PORTIONS
200 g (7 oz) potatoes, peeled and chopped
1 small carrot, peeled and chopped
60 g (2½ oz) broccoli, cut into florets
85 g (3 oz) fillet of salmon
15 g (½ oz) butter
4 tbsp milk
40 g (1½ oz) Cheddar cheese, grated

◉ Put the chopped potato and carrot into a saucepan. Cover with boiling water and cook for 15 minutes, or until the carrots are tender.

◉ Meanwhile, steam the broccoli for about 6 minutes. Cook the salmon either by poaching it in milk or stock until it flakes easily with a fork, or put it into a microwave dish, dot with a knob of butter (take about 5 g/⅛ oz from the 15 g (½ oz) butter in the ingredients). Cover, leaving an air vent and cook for about one and a half minutes.

◉ Mash the cooked potato, carrot and broccoli together with the remaining butter, milk and grated cheese. Finally flake the salmon and stir into the mash.

Chicken with butternut squash and tarragon

Since you can't add salt to baby purées, it's a good idea to add fresh herbs to bring out the flavour.

knob of butter
100 g (3½ oz) onion, finely chopped
100 g (3½ oz) peeled butternut
   squash
100 g (3½ oz) chicken breast
   sliced into small pieces
1 tbsp flour
100 ml (3½ fl oz) milk
⅛ tsp lemon zest
1 tsp lemon juice
1 tbsp Parmesan cheese,
   finely grated
⅛ tsp tarragon, finely chopped

◉ Melt the butter in a saucepan. Add the onion and sauté for 5 minutes, until softened.

◉ Add the butternut squash and chicken and fry for 1–2 minutes.

◉ Sprinkle over the flour, then blend in the milk. Bring up to the boil, stirring until slightly thickened.

◉ Add the zest and juice, cover and simmer for 10 minutes, until the squash is soft and the chicken is cooked.

◉ Purée using a hand blender, then stir in the cheese and tarragon.

Chicken with carrot and apple

When my son was a baby, he refused to eat chicken until I combined it with apple, which he loved.

1 tbsp sunflower oil
60 g (2½ oz) leek, finely chopped
25 g (1 oz) celery, chopped
75 g (3 oz) chopped carrot
1 garlic clove, crushed
100 g (3½ oz) chicken cut into chunks
250 g (9 oz) chopped and peeled sweet potato
75 g (3 oz) chopped apple
250 ml (9 fl oz) boiling unsalted chicken stock or water
sprig of thyme

◉ Heat the oil in a saucepan and sauté the leek for 2 minutes.

◉ Add the celery and carrot and cook for 5 minutes. Add a small clove of crushed garlic and sauté for one minute.

◉ Stir in the chopped chicken and sauté for 2–3 minutes, or until the chicken is sealed.

◉ Add the chopped sweet potato and the apple and pour over the chicken stock or boiling water. Cover and cook over a low heat for 20 minutes.

◉ Remove the sprig of thyme and blitz to a purée.

Creamy chicken with sweet potato 20

A tasty recipe to make with cooked chicken.

SUITABLE FOR FREEZING
SUITABLE FROM 6 MONTHS
MAKES 2 PORTIONS
150 g (5½ oz) sweet potato, peeled and chopped
   (125 g/4½ oz peeled weight)
12 g (¼ oz) butter
1 tbsp flour
150 ml (¼ pint) milk
15 g (½ oz) Cheddar cheese, grated
30 g (1 oz) cooked chicken, chopped

◉ Steam the sweet potato for about 10 minutes, or until tender.

◉ Melt the butter in a small saucepan, stir in the flour to make a roux, then gradually stir in the milk.

◉ Bring to the boil and then reduce the heat and cook for a couple of minutes. Remove from the heat and stir in the grated cheese, until melted.

◉ Whiz the cooked sweet potato together with the diced chicken and cheese sauce.

California chicken 30

Avocado contains more nutrients than any other fruit. They are also rich in monounsaturated fat, the good type of fat which helps prevent heart disease.

NOT SUITABLE FOR FREEZING
SUITABLE FROM 6 MONTHS
MAKES 1 PORTION
30 g (1 oz) cooked chicken, diced
40 g (1½ oz) ripe avocado flesh (about ½ small
   avocado)
2 tbsp natural mild yoghurt (not low fat)
1 tbsp grated Swiss cheese

◉ Simply blend all the ingredients together.

Chicken with tomato and sweet pepper

Adding pure apple juice and sweet potato makes this purée appealing to babies and stirring in the cream cheese gives it a slightly creamier texture.

1 tbsp olive oil
100 g (3½ oz) red pepper, finely diced
50 g (2 oz) sweet potato
100 g (3½ oz) chicken breast, sliced into 2 cm (3/4 in) pieces
1/2 small garlic clove, crushed
100 g (3½ oz) chopped tomatoes
75 ml (2½ fl oz) apple juice
1 tbsp cream cheese

◉ Heat the oil in a saucepan. Add the pepper and sweet potato and sauté for 5 minutes.

◉ Add the chicken and garlic and fry for one minute. Add the tomatoes and apple juice.

◉ Bring to the boil. Cover and simmer for 8 to 10 minutes until soft.

◉ Whizz using a hand blender until smooth. Stir in the cream cheese.

60

SUITABLE FOR FREEZING
SUITABLE FROM 7 MONTHS
MAKES 5 PORTIONS

Beef and carrot casserole

The most easily absorbed source of iron is red meat. Iron is important for your baby's brain development, especially between six months and two years. The iron a baby inherits from its mother runs out at around six months.

200 g (7 oz) minced beef (lean)
1 onion, finely chopped
2 small carrots, roughly chopped
1 stick celery, finely diced
1 tbsp plain flour
50 ml (2 fl oz) apple juice
200 ml (7 fl oz) unsalted beef stock
100 ml (3½ fl oz) passata
1 tsp tomato purée
½ tsp dried thyme
dash of Worcestershire sauce
(optional)
10 g (¼ oz) Parmesan cheese, grated

◉ Heat a saucepan and brown the beef, then add the onion, carrots and celery.

◉ Fry over the heat for 3–4 minutes until lightly browned. Sprinkle over the flour. Blend in the apple juice, stock and passata.

◉ Bring to the boil and add the tomato purée and thyme. Cover with a lid and gently simmer for 30 minutes, until tender.

◉ Add the Worcestershire sauce and Parmesan cheese. Blend to a purée for young babies.

Beef with sweet pepper and tomato purée

This is my baby version of meat and two veg. Don't delay giving meat much beyond 6 months as it provides the best source of iron.

1 tbsp olive oil
100 g (3½ oz) red onion, finely chopped
50 g (2 oz) red pepper, finely diced
50 g (2 oz) sirloin steak, sliced into small thin strips
⅛ tsp ground coriander
200 g (7 oz) chopped tomatoes
2 tsp apple juice

◉ Heat the oil in a saucepan. Add the red onion and pepper and sauté for 5 minutes, until nearly soft.

◉ Add the steak and ground coriander and fry for 2 minutes. Add the tomatoes and apple juice. Cover and simmer for 10 minutes.

◉ Purée using a hand blender until completely smooth.

Cheesy pasta with broccoli and peas

This is a good way to encourage your baby to enjoy greens.

knob of butter
1 small leek, finely chopped
1 tbsp plain flour
250 ml (9 fl oz) milk
40 g (1½ oz) Cheddar cheese, grated
¼ tsp Dijon mustard
75 g (3 oz) small pasta shapes
50 g (2 oz) very small broccoli florets
40 g (1½ oz) frozen petit pois peas

◉ Melt the butter in a saucepan. Add the leek and sauté for 2–3 minutes, until soft. Sprinkle over the flour, then blend in the milk. Bring to the boil, stirring until thickened.

◉ Add the cheese and Dijon mustard. Cook the pasta in boiling water according to the packet instructions.

◉ Add the broccoli to the pasta 5 minutes before the end of the cooking time and cook for 2 minutes. Add the peas and cook for 3–4 minutes. Drain, and mix the pasta with the sauce.

Risotto with tomato and basil

Making a risotto is a good way to introduce texture to a baby's diet.

1 tsp olive oil
1 onion, finely chopped
1 leek, finely chopped
1 clove garlic, crushed
110 g (4 oz) long-grain rice
300 ml (½ pint) water
35 g (1 oz) Parmesan cheese, grated
3 tomatoes, deseeded and chopped
2 tbsp basil, finely chopped

◉ Heat the oil in a saucepan. Add the onion and leek and sauté for 2–3 minutes. Add the garlic and fry for 30 seconds.

◉ Add the rice and coat it in the onion mixture. Pour over the water. Bring up to the boil.

◉ Cover with a lid and simmer over a very low heat for 12–15 minutes or until all of the water is absorbed and the rice is cooked.

◉ Add the cheese, tomatoes and basil. Gently mix together.

First finger foods

Finger foods need to be fairly simple and slightly soft. So until your baby can chew properly, to avoid the risk of choking, give steamed vegetables rather than raw, and soft fruits. Also take care not to give any foods your baby might choke on such as whole grapes or fruits with stones.

Fruits

Start with soft fruits, such as banana, pear, peach, plum, mango, peeled halved grapes, dried apricots and then move on to apple.

Vegetables

Start with steamed vegetables such as carrot sticks, broccoli and cauliflower florets. Once your baby can chew, you can move on to raw vegetables such as cucumber, carrot and sweet pepper sticks.

● ● ● ● ● ● ● ● ● ● ● ● ● ●
TIP
It is often better to give large pieces of fruit or vegetables, which your child can hold and eat rather than bite-sized pieces.

OTHER GOOD FINGER FOODS

◉ Sticks of cheese

◉ Dried fruits, such as apricot or apple

◉ Rice cakes

◉ Pitta bread

◉ Bagels

◉ Dry cereals, but avoid the sugar-coated variety

◉ Toast soldiers spread with peanut butter, cream cheese, pure fruit spread

◉ Fingers of grilled cheese on toast

◉ Mini ice lollies made from fresh fruit or fruit juice (good for sore gums)

Sandwiches

Sandwiches make good finger food and for little ones it is best not to have too much bread or too much filling. It can be a good idea to flatten the bread a little with a rolling pin so that it is easier for small children to handle.

Presentation is important. A child is far more likely to eat something that looks appealing. Try cutting sandwiches into shapes using cookie cutters or use one slice of white and one slice of brown bread to make sandwiches. Remove the crusts and cut into squares, then turn alternate squares over so that you have a chequerboard sandwich.

HERE ARE SOME FAVOURITE SANDWICH FILLINGS TO TRY:

◉ Hummus and finely grated carrot

◉ Mashed tuna mixed with mayonnaise and a little ketchup

◉ Cream cheese and cucumber cut into ribbons using a vegetable peeler

◉ Thinly sliced cheese and ham

◉ Thinly sliced cheese and tomato (remove the seeds so that the bread doesn't become too soggy)

◉ Cream cheese mixed with a little maple syrup and then a layer of mashed banana

◉ Hard-boiled egg mashed with a little mayonnaise and salad cress

◉ Marmite and butter with shredded lettuce

◉ Smoked salmon and cream cheese

◉ Tuna with sweetcorn, spring onion and mayonnaise

◉ Mashed tinned sardines with tomato ketchup

◉ Peanut butter and mashed banana

◉ Peanut butter and low-sugar strawberry jam

◉ Cream cheese and raspberry jam

◉ Cream cheese and chopped dried apricot

◉ Chopped chicken with mayonnaise, sweetcorn and spring onion

Pronto pasta

Fresh tomato sauce with SunBlush tomatoes

This is a good sauce to make when you have some tasty ripe tomatoes to hand. The addition of SunBlush tomatoes enhances the flavour of the tomatoes.

1 tbsp olive oil
1 small onion, finely chopped
1 large clove garlic, crushed
450 g (1 lb) ripe tomatoes, chopped
pinch sugar
¼ tsp balsamic vinegar
250 g (9 oz) small penne pasta
50 g (2 oz) SunBlush tomatoes, chopped

◉ To make the sauce, heat the oil in a saucepan and add the onion and gently simmer for 10 minutes until soft. Then add the garlic and fry for one minute. Next add the tomatoes, sugar and season to taste.

◉ Bring to the boil, then gently simmer for 10–15 minutes, until the tomatoes have broken down. Whiz the sauce with a blender until smooth and then add the vinegar.

◉ Cook the pasta in boiling salted water until it is tender. Drain, toss with the sauce and mix in the SunBlush tomatoes.

Tomato and mascarpone sauce with penne

This makes a lovely creamy tomato sauce, with the mascarpone stirred in.
If you don't have mascarpone you could use cream cheese instead.

1 tbsp olive oil
3 spring onions, thinly sliced
1 clove garlic, crushed
400 g (14 oz) tin chopped tomatoes
5 sunblush tomatoes (packed
   in oil), chopped
2 tbsp tomato purée
2 tbsp tomato ketchup
1½ tsp sugar
200 g (7 oz) penne pasta
4 tbsp mascarpone
salt and pepper

Optional to serve
Parmesan cheese, grated
4 large basil leaves, shredded

◉ Heat the oil in a deep frying pan and sauté the onions and garlic
for 1 minute. Add all of the tomato ingredients plus the sugar,
bring to the boil and simmer briskly for 15 minutes until very thick
(in a wok it may take slightly longer). Meanwhile cook the pasta
according to the packet instructions.

◉ Transfer the sauce to a blender, or bowl, and cool slightly, then
add the mascarpone and blend with the blender or a hand blender
until smooth. Season to taste.

◉ Reserve a cupful of the pasta cooking water before draining the
pasta. Return the pasta to the saucepan and toss with the sauce,
adding 2–3 tbsp of the cooking water if the pasta becomes too dry.
Spoon onto plates and serve with grated Parmesan cheese and
perhaps some fresh basil, if your child likes it.

Spaghetti with pesto

If you are making pesto in advance, make it with 100 ml (3½ fl oz) only of the oil. Transfer to a container and pour the remaining 50 ml (2 fl oz) of oil over the surface. This will stop the pesto from going dark. Store in the fridge and stir before using. Pesto also freezes well in airtight containers for up to 3 months.

75 g (3 oz) pine nuts
50 g (2 oz) fresh basil leaves
1 fat clove garlic
50 g (2 oz) Parmesan cheese, grated
150 ml (1/4 pint) mild olive oil
300 g (10½ oz) spaghetti
salt and pepper

◉ Toast the pine nuts for 2–3 minutes in a dry frying pan (or buy ready-made toasted pine nuts), then leave to cool.

◉ Transfer them to a food processor. Add the basil and garlic and whiz until everything is finely chopped. Then pour in the oil, through the tunnel, with the motor running, until combined.

◉ Add the Parmesan cheese and season to taste, before pulsing for 4–5 minutes to combine. Spoon into a bowl.

◉ Cook the pasta according to the packet instructions. Before draining, reserve a cupful of the cooking water. Mix the pasta with the pesto and add a little cooking water if the pasta gets too dry. Transfer to plates and serve with extra Parmesan cheese.

Pasta primavera

Combining diced vegetables with pasta is a great way to get fussy eaters to have more vegetables in their diet. Simply mix together crème fraîche, stock and parmesan to make a quick, tasty light cheese sauce.

150 g (5½ oz) fusilli pasta
2 tbsp sunflower oil
1 onion, sliced
150 g (5½ oz) butternut squash,
   peeled and diced
½ red pepper, diced (100 g/3½ oz)
1 medium courgette, diced
   (100 g/3½ oz)
100 g (3½ oz) chestnut
   mushrooms, sliced
1 clove garlic, crushed
150 ml (¼ pint) vegetable stock
6 tbsp crème fraîche
60 g (2½ oz) Parmesan cheese,
   grated
2 tbsp basil, chopped
pinch salt

◉ Cook the pasta in boiling water and drain.

◉ Heat the oil in a frying pan. Add the onion and butternut squash and gently fry for 5 minutes. Add the remaining vegetables and fry for 3 minutes. Add the garlic and fry for one minute.

◉ Add the vegetable stock to the pan and let it bubble away until it has reduced by half.

◉ Finally, add the crème fraîche, cheese and basil, then season with a little salt and toss together with the pasta.

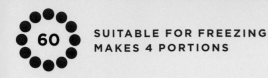

Spinach and tuna lasagne

To save time, you can use a ready-made tomato sauce to make this tasty lasagne. Make sure the top of the lasagne is completely covered with sauce so that the pasta doesn't burn.

1 tbsp olive oil

1 onion, chopped

1 clove garlic, crushed

300 g (10½ oz) pack fresh spinach, washed

150 g (5½ oz) cream cheese

2 x 180 g (6 oz) tins tuna in brine, drained

salt and pepper

500 g (1 lb) container tomato and herb pasta sauce

3 large sheets fresh lasagne (approx 150 g/5½ oz) or 6 small sheets

125 g (4½ oz) ball mozzarella, thinly sliced

2–3 tbsp Parmesan cheese, grated

◉ Pre-heat the oven to 200°C/400°F/Gas 6. Heat the oil in a wok or large frying pan and sauté the onion for 5–6 minutes, until soft.

◉ Add the garlic and spinach and sauté a further 3–4 minutes until the spinach has thoroughly wilted. If your child is fussy you may like to roughly chop the spinach and onion mixture in a food processor, then return to the pan.

◉ Add the cream cheese and stir until melted, then stir in the drained tuna and season to taste.

◉ Put a thick layer of tomato sauce in the bottom of a baking dish about 21 x 15 x 5 cm (8 x 6 x 2 in). Sit a layer of lasagne on the sauce (trim the sheets to fit the dish, if necessary), then spread over half of the tuna mixture. Spoon over a quarter of the tomato sauce, spreading it out slightly, then add another layer of pasta, tuna, and a quarter more of the sauce.

◉ Top with a third layer of pasta and spread over the remaining tomato sauce. Lay over the mozzarella and sprinkle on the Parmesan cheese.

◉ Bake for 40 minutes until the top is browned and slightly puffed.

Cheesy chicken pasta with broccoli

For a vegetarian version, double the amount of broccoli and use vegetable instead of chicken stock.

200 g (7 oz) pasta shapes, e.g. fusilli
100 g (3½ oz) broccoli florets
30 g (1 oz) butter
1 large or 2 small shallots
1 clove garlic, crushed
30 g (1 oz) plain flour
250 ml (9 fl oz) milk
300 ml (½ pint) chicken stock
75 g (3 oz) mature Cheddar cheese, grated
30 g (1 oz) Parmesan cheese, grated
1 cooked chicken breast, shredded (120 g/4 oz)
Sweet smoked Spanish paprika (optional)
salt and pepper

◉ Cook the pasta according to the packet instructions, adding the broccoli for the last 3 minutes.

◉ While the pasta is cooking, melt the butter in a large saucepan and sauté the shallot(s) and garlic for 2–3 minutes, until softening. Add the flour and stir to make a paste, then whisk in the milk and stock to make a smooth sauce – you may find it easier to do this off the heat.

◉ Bring the sauce to the boil, stirring constantly, then remove from the heat and stir in cheeses and chicken.

◉ Drain the pasta and broccoli and return to the pan. Add the sauce and toss to coat, then season to taste. Sweet smoked Spanish paprika adds a delicious flavour to this dish.

Spanish paprika chicken pasta

The paprika adds a nice smoky flavour to this dish.

2 tsp olive oil
1 red onion, finely chopped
½ red pepper, diced
1 clove garlic, crushed
½ tsp smoked Spanish paprika
1 chicken breast, sliced into
　　small pieces
25 g (1 oz) chorizo, roughly chopped
400 g (14 oz) tin chopped tomatoes
½ tsp sundried tomato paste
½ tsp fresh thyme, finely chopped
150 g (5½ oz) shell pasta
75 g (3 oz) mozzarella, cubed

◉ Heat the oil in a saucepan. Add the onion, pepper and garlic and fry gently for 5 minutes. Then add the paprika and chicken and fry for 1 minute.

◉ Mix in the chorizo, then the tomatoes, tomato paste and thyme. Bring to the boil, then simmer for 5 minutes.

◉ Meanwhile, cook the pasta in boiling salted water, drain, then add to the sauce. Mix together, then add the mozzarella.

Macaroni cheese 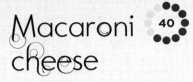 40

This is a delicious macaroni, made with three cheeses.

SUITABLE FOR FREEZING
MAKES 8 PORTIONS
150 g (5½ oz) macaroni
600 ml (1 pint) milk
3 tbsp cornflour
75 g (3 oz) mature cheddar cheese, grated
75 g (3 oz) Gruyère cheese, grated
60 g (2½ oz) Parmesan cheese, grated
125 g (4½ oz) mascarpone
¼ tsp Dijon mustard

For the topping
25 g (1 oz) breadcrumbs (1 slice)
20 g (¾ oz) Parmesan cheese, grated

⦿ Cook the macaroni according to the packet instructions. Drain and rinse under a cold tap. Heat 500 ml (17 fl oz) milk until just boiling.

⦿ Mix the cornflour and the remaining 100 ml (3½ fl oz) milk and whisk into the hot milk. Cook, whisking constantly until the sauce thickens and comes to the boil.

⦿ Whisk in the grated cheeses until melted, then the mascarpone and Dijon mustard. Stir in the cooked pasta and season to taste. Transfer to a baking dish. Mix breadcrumbs and Parmesan cheese and sprinkle over. Grill until golden.

Spaghetti carbonara 30

Carbonara is a perennial favourite with kids of all ages.

NOT SUITABLE FOR FREEZING
MAKES 4 PORTIONS
225 g (8 oz) spaghetti
½ tbsp olive oil
125 g (4½ oz) pancetta, diced
125 ml (4½ fl oz) double cream
2 egg yolks
50 g (2 oz) Parmesan cheese, grated
salt and freshly ground black pepper

⦿ Cook the spaghetti in lightly salted boiling water until al dente.

⦿ Bring a large saucepan of water to the boil. Heat the olive oil in a frying pan and sauté the pancetta for 3–4 minutes, until browned.

⦿ In a bowl, whisk together the cream, egg yolks, Parmesan cheese and salt and pepper. Drain the pasta and return to the saucepan. Immediately stir in the egg and cheese mixture until well combined. Add the pancetta, toss with the sauce and heat through. You can thin the sauce with a little extra cream if necessary. Serve immediately with some freshly grated Parmesan.

Goujons of fish

You can halve the quantities to make four portions.

75 g (3 oz) fresh brown
   breadcrumbs (made from
   3 slices wholemeal bread,
   crusts removed)
45 g (1½ g) Parmesan cheese,
   grated
1 tbsp chopped chives
50 g (2 oz) plain flour, for dusting
1 egg
1 tbsp cold water
pinch salt
2 large lemon soles or plaice,
   skinned and filleted to make
   8 small fillets
2 tbsp sunflower oil for frying

◉ Put the breadcrumbs, cheese and chives in a food processor and whiz to combine. Spread on a plate and spread the flour on a second plate. Beat the egg with the water and salt in a shallow dish.

◉ Cut the fish fillets into strips. Dust the fish fillets with the flour, then dip in egg and coat in breadcrumbs. Lay the cooked fillets on a chopping board or baking sheet.

◉ Heat the oil in a large frying pan. Fry the fillets for 2 minutes each side, until golden. You will probably need to do this in 2–3 batches. Blot with paper towels before serving.

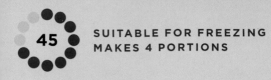
Prawn laksa

The coconut milk makes this a smooth-tasting curry that will go down a treat.

1 onion, thinly sliced
1 tbsp sunflower oil
½ tsp fresh ginger, grated
2 tbsp korma curry paste
   (or 1 tbsp curry powder)
400 ml (14 fl oz) tin coconut milk
200 ml (7 fl oz) chicken, fish
   or vegetable stock
2 tsp soy sauce
1 tsp fish sauce
1 tsp honey
1 large carrot, cut into julienne
   sticks
250 g (9 oz) raw prawns, heads
   and shells removed
100 g (3½ oz) frozen peas
100 g (3½ oz) dry rice noodles,
   prepared according to the packet
   instructions or 250 g (9 oz) fresh
   rice noodles

Optional garnishes
thinly sliced spring onions
coriander leaves
chopped chilli
lime wedges

◉ Sauté the onion in the oil for 5 minutes, until soft. Add the ginger and curry paste and cook for 1 minute. Then add the coconut milk, stock, soy and fish sauce and honey.

◉ Bring to the boil, then reduce the heat, add the carrot and simmer for 5 minutes.

◉ Add the prawns and simmer for 2–3 minutes, until the prawns turn pink. Then add the peas and cook for 1–2 minutes, until the peas have warmed through. Stir in the noodles and ladle into bowls. Finally, if you wish, garnish with one of the suggested options.

60

Tagliatelle with tomato and tuna

I've put olives as optional here as they can be an acquired taste, but I've found many young children really like olives.

1 tbsp olive oil

60 g (2½ oz) red onion, diced

45 g (1½ oz) red pepper, de-seeded and diced

55 g (2 oz) apple, core removed and grated

400 g (14 oz) tin chopped tomatoes

4 tbsp tomato purée

1 tsp sugar

200 ml (7 fl oz) vegetable stock

200 g (7 oz) tagliatelle

2 x 185 g (6½ oz) tins tuna in brine, drained

75 g (3 oz) mature Cheddar cheese, grated

black olives, optional

◉ Heat the oil in a large, deep frying pan and sauté the onion for 3 minutes, until translucent. Add the pepper and cook for a further 5–6 minutes, until the vegetables are soft. Add the apple, tomatoes, tomato purée, sugar and stock and bring to the boil, then simmer for 30 minutes, until thickened.

◉ Blend the sauce until smooth, then return to the pan.

◉ Meanwhile, cook the pasta according to the packet instructions, drain and toss in the sauce. Season with salt and pepper.

◉ Flake the tuna and fold into the pasta.

◉ Transfer to a baking dish and sprinkle over the cheese. Grill until the cheese has melted and is bubbling.

◉ Add a handful of black olives to the tomato sauce, if you like.

Little fish pies with peas

These little fish pies are a great warming dish, and very nutritious.

400 g (14 oz) white potatoes,
   peeled and cubed
30 g (1 oz) butter
2 shallots, finely diced
30 g (1 oz) plain flour
300 ml (½ pint) milk
45 g (1½ oz) Parmesan cheese,
   grated
½ tsp lemon juice
1½ tsp rice wine vinegar
100 g (3½ oz) salmon fillet,
   skinned and cubed
100 g (3½ oz) cod fillet,
   skinned and cubed
40 g (1½ oz) peas, cooked
4 tbsp milk
paprika

◉ Preheat the oven to 180°C/350°F/Gas 4.

◉ First make the mashed potato. Put the cubed potato into cold water. Bring to the boil and simmer for 10–12 minutes until tender. Drain well, then mash.

◉ Melt the butter in a saucepan. Add the shallots and sauté for 5–8 minutes until soft. Add the vinegar, and sauté until most of the vinegar has evaporated. Add the flour and mix together to form a roux. Blend the 300 ml (½ pint) of milk. Stir over gentle heat until thickened.

◉ Remove from the heat and stir in the Parmesan cheese, lemon juice and vinegar. Season and add the cubed fish. Stir in the cooked peas, then spoon into the bases of four 10 cm (4 in) diameter ramekins.

◉ Put the pan of mashed potato back onto the heat. Add the 4 tablespoons of milk and seasoning. Stir until hot, then spoon on top of the fish mixture and fork the top.

◉ Sprinkle with the remaining Parmesan and a little paprika. Place on a baking sheet.

◉ Bake for 15 to 20 minutes until lightly tinged on top and bubbling at the edges

Fusilli with salmon and prawns 25

A simple, light fish dish.

NOT SUITABLE FOR FREEZING
MAKES 4 PORTIONS
250 g (9 oz) fusilli
100 ml (3½ fl oz) fish stock
250 g (9 oz) crème fraîche
juice of ½ lemon (about 2 tbsp)
2 tbsp dill, chopped, plus extra to garnish
150 g (5½ oz) prawns, cooked
150 g (5½ oz) salmon, cooked
1–2 tomatoes, skinned and diced (optional)

◉ Cook the pasta following the packet instructions. Reserve one cup of the pasta cooking water, then drain the pasta and set aside.

◉ Put the stock in a pan and boil until reduced by half. Reduce the heat to low, stir in the crème fraîche, lemon juice and dill. Add the salmon and prawns and warm through, then add the pasta and carefully toss together, adding a splash of the reserved pasta water if the sauce gets too thick.

◉ Stir in the tomatoes (if using). Season with a little salt and pepper and serve immediately, sprinkled with extra dill.

Salmon with Parmesan crust and tomato salsa 25

The salsa adds a nice juiciness to this recipe.

NOT SUITABLE FOR FREEZING
MAKES 4 PORTIONS
50 g (2 oz) fresh white breadcrumbs
15 g (½ oz) Parmesan cheese, freshly grated
1 tbsp chives, chopped finely
50 g (2 oz) plain flour
500 g (1 lb) middle-cut salmon, skinned
1 egg, beaten
2 tbsp olive oil

For the salsa
3 large tomatoes, deseeded and roughly chopped
2 tbsp basil, chopped
3 spring onions, thinly sliced
1 tbsp olive oil
1 tbsp rice wine vinegar
pinch sugar (optional)

◉ Mix the breadcrumbs, cheese and chives together. Spread on a plate. Put the flour onto another plate.

◉ Slice the salmon into 8 pieces. Toss each piece in the flour, then egg and then coat in the breadcrumbs. Heat the oil in a frying pan. Fry the salmon fingers for 3–4 minutes each side until golden and crispy and cooked through.

To make the salsa
Measure all the ingredients into a mixing bowl and toss together. Serve with the salmon.

Sweet chilli salmon and simple stir-fry noodles

Children may prefer to have the salmon broken into large flakes or cut into cubes and tossed through the noodles.

For the noodles
1 small onion, thinly sliced
1 tbsp sunflower oil
½ tsp fresh ginger, grated
1 clove garlic, crushed
100 g (3½ oz) bean sprouts
   or your favourite stir-fry
   vegetable mixture
100 g (3½ oz) dry Chinese noodles,
   prepared according to packet
   instructions, or 200 g (7 oz)
   fresh noodles
1 tbsp soy sauce
1 tsp sesame oil

For the salmon
2 tbsp sweet chilli sauce
1 tsp rice wine vinegar
1 tsp honey
1 tsp soy sauce
½ tsp fresh ginger, grated
2 x 100 g (3½ oz) skinless,
   boneless salmon fillets

◉ Heat the oil in a wok and stir-fry the onion for 4–5 minutes until soft and slightly browned. Add the ginger and garlic and fry for 1 minute, then add the bean sprouts or stir-fry vegetables and cook for 2 minutes, until the vegetables start to soften.

◉ Add the noodles and cook for 1–2 minutes to reheat, then stir in the soy sauce and sesame oil and set aside.

◉ Preheat the grill to high and line the grill pan with foil. Mix together the sweet chilli sauce, vinegar, honey, soy sauce and ginger.

◉ Grill the skinned side of the salmon for 2 minutes, then turn over and spoon 1 teaspoon of the sweet chilli glaze on the top of each piece of the salmon, spreading it out and down the sides slightly.

◉ Grill for 2 minutes, spread a further teaspoon glaze on each salmon fillet and grill for a further 3–6 minutes, until the salmon is cooked through and the top is glazed and slightly caramelised at the edges.

◉ Add the leftover glaze to the noodles and stir-fry over high heat for about 2 minutes until piping hot. Serve with the salmon.

Bag baked trout with ginger soy

Trout is an oily fish, so it's a good source of omega-3. It has a milder flavour than salmon, so it's a good fish to try, as children find salmon a little overpowering. Baking fish in parcels seals in all the nutrients and flavour.

sunflower oil for greasing
1 small rainbow trout, filleted
   and pin bones removed
6 thin slices fresh ginger
1 tsp soy sauce
1 tsp rice wine vinegar
1 tbsp water

For the dressing
1 tbsp sunflower oil
2 spring onions, finely chopped
½ tsp grated fresh ginger
1 tsp soy sauce
1 tsp rice wine vinegar
½ tsp sesame oil
½ tsp clear honey

PIN BONES
Filleted trout will often have pin bones and these must be removed for children. This is very easy to do. Run your finger down the flesh side of the fillet – you will feel the pin bones. You can easily pluck them out using a pair of tweezers.

◉ Preheat the oven to 200°C/400°F/Gas 6, with a baking sheet in the oven.

◉ Cut 2 large pieces of foil or baking parchment and grease with sunflower oil. Lay the fish fillets on the foil/parchment and place 3 slices of ginger on each one.

◉ Mix the soy sauce, vinegar and water together and spoon over the fish. Wrap the foil/parchment to form a parcel, scrunching the foil or using metal paper clips to help secure the parchment. Put on the baking sheet and bake for 10 minutes.

◉ Meanwhile, heat the sunflower oil in a small frying pan. Add the onions and ginger and when they start to sizzle, take the frying pan off the heat and set aside.

◉ Unwrap the fish parcels and remove the ginger. Transfer the fish to plates, using a fish slice or palette knife and sliding it between the fish and the skin to remove the skin from the cooked fish.

◉ Pour any juices left in the foil/parchment into the frying pan, then add the soy sauce, vinegar, sesame oil and honey. Stir together, then spoon over the fish and serve immediately.

Asian rice salad with prawns 20

NOT SUITABLE FOR FREEZING
MAKES 3 PORTIONS
100 g (3½ oz) jasmine rice
¼ red pepper, diced
3 tbsp drained, tinned sweetcorn
2 spring onions, thinly sliced
100 g (3½ oz) small cooked prawns
coriander leaves, to garnish

For the dressing
2 tbsp rice wine vinegar
2 tsp sugar
1 tsp mirin
1 tsp sunflower oil

◉ Cook the rice according to the package instructions. Drain, rinse with cold water and then leave to drain in a sieve for 10 minutes. Then transfer to a bowl.

◉ Stir in the pepper, sweetcorn, onions and prawns.

◉ Whisk together the dressing ingredients. Pour over the salad and stir it in.

◉ Cover and chill. Serve decorated with coriander leaves.

Oriental cod balls with plum dipping sauce 25

SUITABLE FOR FREEZING
MAKES ABOUT 20 BALLS
250 g (9 oz) cod fillet, skinned
1 bunch spring onions, finely chopped
1½ tbsp sweet chilli sauce
25 g (1 oz) Parmesan cheese, grated
1 tsp soy sauce
1 egg yolk
25 g (1 oz) Japanese dried breadcrumbs
2 tbsp sunflower oil

For the sauce
3 tbsp plum sauce
2 tbsp water
2 tsp soy sauce

◉ Whiz the cod in a food processor, until roughly chopped, then transfer to a bowl.

◉ Add the spring onions, chilli sauce, cheese, soy sauce, egg yolk and breadcrumbs and mix together. Shape into 20 balls.

◉ Heat the oil in a frying pan. Fry the balls for about 8–10 minutes, until lightly golden and cooked through.

To make the sauce
◉ Measure all the sauce ingredients into a small saucepan. Gently warm through and serve with the balls.

Mild korma curry with prawns

Curry is one of my children's favourite meals, and this is a mild and fruity version. Serve with poppadums and rice.

2 tbsp olive oil
1 small onion, finely chopped
1 tsp ginger, grated
1 tbsp korma curry paste
1 tsp garam masala
225 g (8 oz) tin chopped tomatoes
250 ml (9 fl oz) coconut milk
½ tsp lemon juice
½ –1 tsp mango chutney
200 g (7 oz) raw king prawns, peeled
salt and pepper

◉ Heat the oil in a saucepan. Add the onion and sauté for 3 minutes. Add the ginger, curry paste and garam masala and fry for 2 minutes.

◉ Add the tomatoes, coconut milk, lemon juice and mango chutney. Bring to the boil, then simmer, uncovered, for about 8–10 minutes, stirring until it has reduced and is an orange-red colour.

◉ Season and add the prawns and cook for another 5 minutes, until they have turned pink and are cooked through.

Express chicken and poultry

Quick sauces for chicken

Serve these sauces with griddled or pan-fried chicken.

Griddled chicken

NOT SUITABLE FOR FREEZING
MAKES 2 PORTIONS
2 chicken breasts
1 tbsp olive or sunflower oil
1 clove garlic, peeled
a little salt and pepper

◉ Cover the chicken breast fillets with clingfilm and bash with a mallet to flatten them.

◉ Brush the fillets with oil and then run a cut garlic clove over them. Season with a little salt and pepper.

◉ Brush a griddle pan with oil and when it is very hot cook the chicken on one side for 2–3 minutes. Then turn the heat down a little and cook for a further 3 minutes. Turn the chicken over and repeat on the other side.

◉ Cut the chicken into strips and simply mix all the ingredients together to make tasty dipping sauces for the chicken.

SAUCES
Mild curry

2 tbsp mayonnaise
2 tbsp Greek yoghurt
1½ tsp mild korma curry paste
1 tsp clear honey
2–3 drops lemon juice

Easy barbecue

3 tbsp tomato ketchup
1 tbsp clear honey
¼ tsp soy sauce
¼ tsp lemon juice
2 tsp water

Spicy tomato

3 tbsp tomato ketchup
1 tbsp sweet chilli sauce
1 tbsp water
¼ tsp soy sauce

◉ Simply mix all the ingredients together for your sauce of choice, and paste on the chicken before cooking.

Chicken bolognese

If your child is a fussy eater and picks out the vegetables, cook them until they are soft, add the tomatoes and blend until smooth. Brown the chicken in a separate frying pan and add the remaining ingredients before simmering as per the recipe.

1 tbsp olive oil
1 onion, finely chopped
¼ red pepper, diced
1 medium carrot (60 g/2½ oz) peeled and diced
½ small stalk celery, diced (optional)
1 clove garlic, crushed
¼ tsp thyme leaves, chopped
250 g (9 oz) minced chicken
400 g (14 oz) can chopped tomatoes
150 ml (¼ pint) chicken stock
2 tbsp tomato purée
1 tbsp sundried tomato purée or ketchup
1½ tsp sugar

◉ Heat the oil in a large saucepan. Sauté the vegetables for 8–10 minutes until soft, then add the garlic and thyme and cook for one minute.

◉ Add the chicken and turn up the heat slightly, then cook for 2–4 minutes, stirring, and breaking up the chicken with a wooden spoon until the chicken has coloured slightly.

◉ Add the remaining ingredients, bring to the boil, then reduce the heat and simmer for 20–30 minutes until thickened. Season with salt and pepper.

Little chicken and leek pies

Little ones will love to have mini-sized portions in individual ramekin dishes. You can also prepare several at a time and freeze extra portions for days when you don't have time to cook.

225 g (8 oz) peeled potatoes, diced
225 g (8 oz) carrots, diced
20 g (¾ oz) butter
2 small leeks, roughly chopped
2 chicken breasts, skinned and
    sliced into 2 cm (¾ in) cubes
3 mushrooms, sliced
2 level tbsp plain flour
200 ml (7 fl oz) milk
50 g (2 oz) Cheddar, grated
25 g (1 oz) sweetcorn

◉ Preheat the grill.

◉ Put the potatoes and carrots into a saucepan. Bring to the boil and keep it there for 10–12 minutes, until soft. Drain, then mash until smooth.

◉ Melt the butter in a saucepan. Add the leeks and sauté for 5 minutes, until just soft. Add the chicken and fry for 2 minutes. Next, add the mushrooms and cook for 2 minutes. Sprinkle over the plain flour. Blend in the milk and bring up to the boil.

◉ Gently simmer for 5 minutes, until the chicken is cooked. Add three-quarters of the cheese, seasoning and sweetcorn. Spoon into 4 size-1 ramekins. Spoon the mash on top and sprinkle with the remaining cheese.

◉ Grill for 4–5 minutes, until lightly golden on top and bubbling around the edges.

Chicken with ham and cheese

This recipe is a delicious way to stuff chicken breasts.

4 small chicken breasts, skinned
80 g (3 oz) Gruyère cheese, grated
4 small slices ham, finely chopped
4 tbsp chives, snipped
1 egg, beaten
50 g (2 oz) fresh breadcrumbs
paprika
2 tbsp oil

◉ Preheat the oven to 200°C/400°/Gas 6

◉ Put the chicken breasts onto a board. Cover with clingfilm and, using a mallet, lightly bash the thicker part of the breast so that it is roughly the same thickness.

◉ Carefully slice each breast three-quarters of the way through the middle, still keeping one side attached. Mix the cheese, ham and chives together.

◉ Open the breast and put a quarter of the cheese mixture into the middle. Season and fold over the top. Push down so that it looks like a sandwich.

◉ Brush with egg wash. Carefully coat in breadcrumbs. Sprinkle with paprika.

◉ Heat the oil in a large frying pan. Brown the breast for 3 minutes on both sides, then place onto a baking sheet lined with non-stick paper.

◉ Roast in the oven for 15 minutes until golden and cooked through. Leave for 3 minutes, then slice each breast into 3–4 slices to serve.

Chicken and gravy casserole

You could bash the chicken to flatten it and then marinate in olive oil, garlic and lemon (see p.84 for instructions on griddling).

2 tsp olive oil
2 chicken breasts, sliced into strips
2 onions, thinly sliced
1 tsp thyme, finely chopped
pinch brown sugar
1 tsp balsamic vinegar
300 ml (½ pint) beef stock
½ tsp Worcestershire sauce
¼ tsp tomato purée
2 level tsp cornflour

◉ Heat the oil in a deep frying pan. Season the chicken. Brown the chicken on both sides until lightly golden, then set aside on a plate.

◉ Add the onions to the pan. Sprinkle over the thyme. Cover and gently simmer for about 8–10 minutes, until very soft. Remove the lid, add the sugar and balsamic vinegar and fry until lightly golden.

◉ Add the stock, Worcestershire sauce and tomato purée. Bring up to the boil. Mix the cornflour with a little cold water then add to the gravy. Stir until thickened.

◉ Return the chicken to the pan. Cover and gently simmer for 4–5 minutes until cooked through. Serve with mashed potatoes.

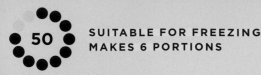
Chicken meatballs in barbecue sauce

This is one of my children's favourite recipes. It's a good idea to make extra and pop some child-sized portions into the freezer so that they're there whenever you need them.

1 tbsp olive oil
1 onion, finely chopped
1 clove garlic, crushed
100 ml (3½ fl oz) ketchup
400 ml (14 fl oz) water
1½ tbsp soy sauce
1 tbsp brown sugar
2 tsp Worcestershire sauce
1 tsp balsamic vinegar
1 tsp lemon juice
1 tbsp cornflour

For the meatballs
2 chicken breasts, skinned
1 slice white bread
2 tsp fresh thyme, chopped
1 egg yolk
1 apple, peeled and grated

◉ Heat the oil in a saucepan. Add the onion and garlic and simmer for 5 minutes, until soft.

◉ Divide the mixture into two and put half in a mixing bowl. Add the ketchup, water, soy sauce, brown sugar, Worcestershire sauce and balsamic vinegar to the pan. Bring to the boil and simmer for 2 minutes.

◉ Add the lemon juice. Mix the cornflour with a little cold water and add to the sauce, then stir until thickened.

To make the meatballs

◉ Chop up the chicken in a food processor until it is finely chopped. Whiz the slice of bread in a food processor to make fine breadcrumbs.

◉ Put the breadcrumbs and minced chicken into the mixing bowl with the remaining onion. Add the thyme, egg yolk and apple and mix together. Shape into 24 balls.

◉ Heat a little oil in a frying pan. Fry the balls until lightly golden. Add to the sauce and simmer for 5–8 minutes, until cooked through.

Toasted chicken tortilla

It's a nice idea to cook filled tortillas on a griddle to make them crispy. They make great finger food.

180 g (6 oz) chicken breast, skinned and sliced into thin strips
1 tsp runny honey
2 tbsp olive oil
3 spring onions, finely sliced
25 g (1 oz) Cheddar cheese, grated
3 tbsp tinned sweetcorn
2 tbsp fresh basil, roughly chopped
4 tbsp light mayonnaise
4 tortilla wraps

◉ Put the chicken into a bowl. Drizzle over the honey and season. Heat 1 tablespoon of oil in a small frying pan and fry the chicken for 4–6 minutes until cooked, then set aside.

◉ Measure the spring onions, cheddar cheese, basil, sweetcorn, mayonnaise and seasoning into a small bowl. Slice the chicken into small pieces, then add to the mixture and mix together.

◉ Heat a griddle pan until hot. Put the tortillas in the pan and gently warm through so that they are easier to roll. Place one on a work surface. Put a quarter of the mixture on one side of the tortilla, roll up, making sure that the end is underneath. Repeat with the remaining tortillas.

◉ Brush both sides with a little oil, then fry on both sides until char-grilled and the filling is warm and the cheese is starting to melt.

Marinated griddled chicken

Cut the marinated, griddled chicken into strips and serve with a selection of vegetables, depending on what your child likes.

For the marinade
1 tbsp sunflower oil
1 tsp balsamic vinegar
2 tsp honey
1 tsp sesame oil
1 tsp soy sauce

For the chicken
1 large chicken breast
¼ red pepper, cut into 2
    lengthways
¼ yellow pepper, cut into
    2 lengthways
2½ cm (1 in) piece courgette
    cut into 6 slices

◉ Whisk the marinade ingredients together in a bowl. Cut the chicken in half crosswise. Put the two slices on a board, cover with clingfilm and beat until about a ½ cm (¼ in) thick. Transfer to a bowl. Put the vegetables in a separate bowl.

◉ Divide the marinade between the chicken and vegetables. Toss so that the chicken and vegetables are coated. Cover and marinate for 30 minutes (up to 1 hour).

◉ Heat a griddle pan, brush with a little oil and cook the courgettes 1– 1½ minutes each side. Cook the peppers 3–4 minutes each side and the chicken for 2–3 minutes each side or until the vegetables are soft and the chicken is cooked through.

◉ Transfer the marinade from the bowls to a saucepan. Bring to the boil and boil for 30 seconds, then spoon over the chicken and vegetables.

◉ Do not serve the marinade without boiling first.

Tasty baked chicken

You can also make this recipe using chicken drumsticks, just remove some of the skin and trim away any excess fat.

For the mango chutney glaze
4 tbsp mango chutney
1 tbsp rice wine vinegar
   (or lemon juice)
1 tbsp tomato ketchup
Pinch salt

For the sticky soy and ginger
4 tbsp clear honey
2 tbsp soy sauce
1 tbsp rice wine vinegar
1 clove garlic, crushed
1 tsp grated fresh ginger
1 tbsp sunflower oil

◉ Preheat the oven to 200°C/400°/Gas 6.

◉ Whisk the coating ingredients together. Put the thighs in an ovenproof baking dish or tin and make 2 cuts in each.

◉ Season with pepper, then spoon over the coating. Cover with foil and bake for 15 minutes.

◉ Uncover, baste with the pan juices and bake for a further 15–20 minutes (if possible, baste again after 10 minutes) until the chicken is cooked through and the pan juices are sticky.

◉ Transfer the chicken to a plate and spoon over the pan juices. Cool slightly before serving with rice or baked potatoes and green salad.

Fruity chicken korma

This is a delicious, mild, fruity curry.

1½ tbsp sunflower oil
1 medium onion, finely chopped
½ red pepper, diced
1 small to medium apple, peeled
  and finely sliced
2 chicken breasts, sliced into 2 cm
  (¾ in) cubes
1½ tbsp korma curry paste
1 tsp garam masala
100 ml (¼ pint) low-fat
  coconut milk
100 ml (3½ fl oz) chicken stock
1–1½ tbsp mango chutney
1 tbsp soy sauce
6 baby corn, sliced on the diagonal
50 g (2 oz) frozen peas
2 tsp lime juice
1 tsp cornflour

◉ Heat the oil in a deep-frying pan or wok.

◉ Add the onion and red pepper and stir-fry for 3 minutes. Next, add the apple slices and sauté for 2 minutes. Add the chicken and stir-fry until sealed. Add the curry paste and garam masala, then the coconut milk, stock, mango chutney, soy sauce and baby corn.

◉ Bring to the boil and simmer for 3 minutes. Add the peas and lime juice and cook for 2–3 minutes. Mix the cornflour with 2 tbsp of cold water. Add to the curry and stir until slightly thickened. Serve with rice.

SUITABLE FOR FREEZING
MAKES 4 PORTIONS

Thai green curry

Thai curry paste can differ in strength – the one I use is quite milky, but if you have a hot variety, then you may need to adjust the quantity to suit your child's tastes.

1 tbsp sunflower oil
1 onion, thinly sliced
1 clove garlic, crushed
2–3 tsp soy sauce or fish sauce, to taste
2–3 tsp green curry paste, to taste
1½ tsp sugar
400 ml (14 oz) can low-fat coconut milk
½ vegetable stock cube
85 g (3 oz) small broccoli florets
2 skinless boneless chicken breasts, cut into strips
50 g (2 oz) mangetout, cut into matchsticks
rind of ½ lime (1 tbsp)
3 spring onions, thinly sliced
handful of coriander leaves, to serve

◉ Heat the oil in a wok. Sauté the onion for 4–5 minutes, until soft. Add the garlic, 2 tablespoons of soy or fish sauce, curry paste (to taste), sugar and cook for 1 minute.

◉ Add the coconut milk and stir in the stock cube until dissolved. Bring to the boil, add the broccoli and chicken and gently simmer for 5 minutes. Add the mangetout and simmer for 2 minutes more.

◉ Stir in the lime juice, spring onion and extra soy or fish sauce, if needed. Serve with white rice and garnish with coriander and extra lime wedges, if liked.

Honey and soy-glazed drumsticks

You can marinate the chicken overnight if you have the time.

1 tsp fresh ginger, finely grated
2 tsp soy sauce
1 tsp runny honey
1 tsp olive oil
4 small chicken drumsticks

◉ Preheat the oven to 200°C/400°/Gas 6. Measure the ginger, soy, honey and oil into a bowl. Mix well. Line a baking sheet with non-stick paper.

◉ It is important to score the drumsticks before you marinate them so that they cook all the way through. Put the drumsticks into the marinade. Toss together and season. Tip onto the baking sheet. Roast for 20–30 minutes, turning halfway through. Remove from the baking sheet, wrap the ends in foil and serve.

Jambalaya

The beauty of this dish is that you can substitute or add any ingredients you wish, so it's a great way of using up leftovers. If you like spicy food sauté 50 g (2 oz) diced chorizo with the vegetables and remove the paprika.

1 tbsp olive oil
1 onion, finely chopped
1 medium carrot, peeled and diced
¼ red pepper, diced
½ stick celery, diced
1 clove garlic, crushed
¼ tsp thyme leaves
½ tsp paprika
200 g (7 oz) basmati, or
    long-grain rice
400 g (14 oz) tin chopped tomatoes
250 ml (9 fl oz) chicken stock
4 to 6 drops Tabasco, or to taste
1 cooked chicken breast, about
    120 g (4½ oz)
100 g (3½ oz) cooked prawns
75 g (3 oz) frozen peas
150 g (5½ oz) tinned sweetcorn,
    drained

◉ Heat the oil in a large saucepan or wok with a lid.

◉ Sauté the onion, carrot, pepper and celery for 8–10 minutes, until soft.

◉ Add the garlic, thyme and paprika and cook for one minute. Then add the rice, tomatoes, stock and Tabasco and bring to the boil. Cover and simmer for 15 minutes, or until the rice is just tender.

◉ Uncover and add the chicken, prawns, peas and sweetcorn. Reduce the heat to low, cover and cook for a further 5 minutes, until everything is hot. Season and stir with a fork. Serve with extra Tabasco, if you wish.

Barbecue beef Sloppy Joe

It's best to cook the mince for 30 minutes as it makes it more tender. You could also chop the mince in a food processor for a few seconds.

1 tbsp olive oil
1 medium red onion, chopped
1 clove garlic, crushed
1 tbsp balsamic vinegar
250 g (9 oz) lean beef, minced
400 g (14 oz) tin chopped tomatoes
4 tbsp tomato ketchup
½ tsp Worcestershire sauce
½ tsp soy sauce
1 tsp soft light brown sugar
salt and pepper

◉ Heat the oil in a large frying pan with high sides or a wok. Sauté the onion and garlic for 5 minutes, add the vinegar and the beef and cook for 2 minutes, stirring until the beef no longer looks raw, then add the remaining ingredients.

◉ Bring to the boil, then reduce the heat and simmer for 25–30 minutes. Season to taste. Add a splash of water if the sauce gets too dry. It should be slightly sloppy (hence the name).

To serve
◉ Sloppy Joe is usually served in a split hamburger bun, but you could also serve it with rice. Cook 150 g (5½ oz) rice according to the packet instructions. Drain, spoon onto plates and then top with the meat sauce.

Quick Bolognese

Always a favourite – and the recipe below is a quick and easy way to make bolognese.

1 tbsp olive oil
1 onion, chopped
1 clove garlic, crushed
1 medium carrot, peeled and grated
¼ red pepper, roughly chopped
400 g (14 oz) tin chopped tomatoes
2 tbsp tomato purée
250 g (9 oz) lean minced beef
1 tsp sugar
salt and pepper

◉ Heat the oil in a large frying pan with high sides, or a wok, and sauté the onion and garlic for 5 minutes, until the onion is translucent.

◉ Meanwhile, whiz the carrot, red pepper and tinned tomatoes to a purée in a food processor.

◉ Add the beef to the frying pan and cook for 2 minutes, until it no longer looks raw, then add the tomato mixture, tomato purée and sugar. Bring to the boil, then simmer for 25 minutes, stirring occasionally. Add a splash of water if the sauce gets too dry. Season to taste with salt and pepper.

To serve with pasta
◉ While the sauce is simmering, bring a large saucepan of salted water to the boil, add 200 g (7 oz) pasta and boil for the time specified on the package. Drain and stir into the sauce at the end of the cooking time. Serve with grated Parmesan cheese.

◉ Reserve a little of the pasta cooking water and add a splash if the sauce and pasta get too dry.

Annabel's goulash express

A delicious quick way to make a tasty goulash. Serve with noodles or rice.

350 g (12 oz) sirloin steak, trimmed of fat
1 tbsp olive oil
1 onion, chopped
1 clove garlic, crushed
½ red pepper, deseeded, cut into matchsticks
1 tsp paprika
¼ tsp smoked paprika
400 g (14 oz) tin chopped tomatoes
2 tbsp tomato purée
125 ml (4½ fl oz) beef stock
½ tsp sugar
salt and pepper
2 tbsp crème fraîche or soured cream
1 tbsp fresh parlsey, chopped (optional)

◉ Put the steak on a chopping board, cover with clingfilm and beat with a mallet or rolling pin until 3 mm (⅛ in) thick. Cut into strips the size of a little finger.

◉ Heat the oil in a wok or large frying pan. Sear the beef for 3 minutes; it should still be pink inside. Transfer the beef to a plate and set aside.

◉ Return the wok to the heat and add the onion, garlic and red pepper. Sauté for 2 minutes until soft, then add paprika and sauté for a further 3 minutes.

◉ Add both tomatoes and purée, stock and sugar, bring to the boil and simmer for 10 minutes. Turn the heat to very low, add the beef to the wok and cook very gently for 5 minutes. Try not to boil the sauce once the beef has been added.

◉ Remove from the heat, season to taste and stir in the crème fraîche. Sprinkle over the parsley, if using.

To serve with the goulash
◉ Buttered noodles are a common accompaniment. Cook 200 g (7 oz) tagliatelle according to the packet instructions, drain and toss with a knob of butter. Divide between 3–4 plates and spoon over the goulash.

◉ Alternatively cook 150 g (5½ oz) rice according to the packet instructions, drain and divide between 3–4 plates, then spoon over the goulash.

Mild massaman beef curry

Massaman curry comes from southern Thailand and is one of the few Thai curries made with beef.

350 g (12 oz) sirloin steak, trimmed of fat
1 tbsp sunflower oil
1 onion, chopped
1 clove garlic, crushed
½ tsp ground coriander
½ tsp ground cumin
½ tsp fresh ginger, grated
2 tsp red Thai curry paste, or to taste
8 small new potatoes (200 g/7 oz), cut into quarters
400 ml (14 fl oz) can coconut milk
125 ml (4½ fl oz) beef stock
1 tsp soy sauce
1 tsp sugar
2 tsp lime juice
1 tbsp fresh coriander, chopped (optional)
1 tbsp chopped peanuts (optional)
wedge of lime (optional)
mangetout, cut into matchsticks (optional)

◉ Put the steak on a chopping board. Cover with a piece of clingfilm and beat with a mallet or rolling pin until it is 3 mm (⅛ in) thick. Cut into pieces the size of a little finger.

◉ Heat the oil in a wok and sear the beef for 2–3 minutes. It should still be pink inside. Transfer to a plate and set aside.

◉ Return the wok to the heat and sauté the onion, garlic, coriander and cumin for 5 minutes. Add the ginger, curry paste, potatoes, coconut milk, stock, soy sauce and sugar and bring to the boil and simmer rapidly for 10 minutes, or until the potatoes are tender.

◉ Turn the heat down to low and cook for a further 5 minutes. Try not to let the curry boil once the meat has been added. Stir in the lime juice. Taste after the first teaspoon has been added and add more if you like. Sprinkle over the chopped coriander, if using.

To serve the curry
◉ Traditionally the curry is served in bowls sprinkled with chopped coriander and peanuts, with a wedge of lime to squeeze over it and some poppadoms.

◉ If you prefer to serve with rice, then omit the potatoes and just simmer the sauce for 10 minutes without potatoes in it. Cook 150 g (5½ oz) rice according to the packet instructions.

◉ Add a handful of mangetout, cut into matchsticks and add the beef to the curry for the last 5 minutes' cooking time. Drain the rice, divide between bowls and spoon over the finished curry.

Thyme, garlic and lemon lamb chops

These marinated lamb chops are beautifully tender.

4 sprigs fresh thyme
1 clove garlic, crushed
2 tsp lemon juice
2 tbsp olive oil
4 lamb chops

◉ Pull the leaves from the thyme sprigs and put in a bowl with the lemon juice, garlic and oil. Add the chops and coat in the marinade. Marinate for as long as possible.

◉ Put onto a baking sheet and grill about 20 cm (8 in) away from a hot grill for 8–10 minutes, turning over halfway through the cooking time. This makes a 'pink' chop.

◉ Cook for 12–15 minutes for well-done chop.

Speedy veg

Garlic pitta breadsticks ● 10

Crudités served with delicious home-made breadsticks make wonderful finger food.

SUITABLE FOR FREEZING
MAKES 20 STICKS
4 large pitta breads
30 g (1 oz) butter, softened
1 small clove garlic, crushed
2 tbsp pesto
4 heaped tbsp Parmesan cheese, finely grated

◉ Pre-heat the grill to high. Arrange the pitta breads on a baking sheet. Mix the butter, garlic and pesto together. Spread over one side of the pitta breads.

◉ Sprinkle over the cheese. Grill for 4–5 minutes until golden brown and bubbling.

◉ Leave to cool then slice into sticks.

Sundried tomato sticks ● 10

NOT SUITABLE FOR FREEZING
MAKES 20 STICKS
4 large pitta breads
4 heaped tbsp sun-dried tomato paste
4 heaped tbsp Parmesan cheese, finely grated

◉ Preheat the grill to its highest setting. Arrange the pitta breads on a baking sheet.

◉ Spread the sundried tomato paste over one side. Sprinkle with the cheese and grill for 4–5 minutes, until golden and crisp.

◉ Leave to cool, then slice into 5 sticks.

Dips

Serve with cucumber, carrot, sweet pepper sticks, pitta bread and cherry tomatoes and try some more unusual vegetables, such as sweet sugar snap peas, for dipping.

Sweet chilli and cream cheese dip

NOT SUITABLE FOR FREEZING
100 g (3½ oz) light cream cheese
1 tsp chives, chopped
1 tsp sweet chilli sauce

◉ Mix the cream cheese and chives and put in a ramekin. Spoon over the chilli sauce, or mix together if you prefer.

Thousand island

NOT SUITABLE FOR FREEZING
2 tbsp Greek yoghurt
2 tbsp mayonnaise
2 tsp ketchup
½ tsp lemon juice
1–2 drops Worcestershire sauce

Ranch dip

NOT SUITABLE FOR FREEZING
3 tbsp sour cream
2 tbsp mayonnaise
1 tsp lime (optional)
1 tsp coriander, chopped
1 tsp chives, chopped

Mango and cream cheese dip

NOT SUITABLE FOR FREEZING
4 tbsp low-fat cream cheese
3 tbsp natural yoghurt
1½ tbsp mango chutney
1 tbsp lemon juice
pinch curry powder

◉ Mix all of the ingredients together in a bowl.

◉ Season to taste and serve with breadsticks.

Tomato and cheese quesadilla

20

A few drops of Tabasco sauce add a bit of kick to these quesadillas, but they are still very mild.

NOT SUITABLE FOR FREEZING
MAKES 2 PORTIONS
1 tsp sunflower oil
2 spring onions, thinly sliced
6 large, or 10 small, cherry tomatoes, roughly chopped
3–4 drops Tabasco sauce
2 flour tortilla wraps
55 g (2 oz) Cheddar cheese, grated
salt and pepper

◉ Heat the oil in a saucepan or small frying pan. Add the onions and tomatoes and sauté for 3–4 minutes, until the tomatoes are soft.

◉ Remove from the heat and stir in the Tabasco sauce and season to taste. Heat a large griddle or non-stick frying pan.

◉ Spread the tomato over one of the wraps and scatter over the cheese.

◉ Sandwich with the second wrap and cook in the hot pan for 2–3 minutes each side, until the cheese has melted. Transfer to a board and cut into 12 wedges.

Caramelised onion quesadilla

35

Sweet caramelised onions make a delicious filling for quesadillas.

NOT SUITABLE FOR FREEZING
MAKES 2 PORTIONS
1 tbsp olive oil
1 large or 2 small red onions, thinly sliced
½ tsp fresh thyme leaves (optional)
1 tbsp balsamic vinegar
1 tsp soft light brown sugar
2 flour tortilla wraps
55 g (2 oz) Cheddar cheese, grated
salt and pepper

◉ Heat the oil in a small frying pan. Add the onion and thyme (if using) and cook over medium heat for 15 minutes, until the onion is soft.

◉ Increase the heat to high and add the vinegar and sugar. Cook, stirring until the vinegar has evaporated. Remove from the heat and season to taste. Cool slightly.

◉ Heat a large non-stick frying pan or griddle pan. Spread the onions over one of the wraps and scatter the cheese over.

◉ Sandwich with the second wrap, then griddle for 2–3 minutes either side, until the cheese has melted or cook in the frying pan. Transfer to a board and cut into 12 wedges.

Tasty veggie burrito

These make the most delicious meal and it's easy to double the quantity. Simply make two separate omelettes and just cook double the amount of filling.

1 soft tortilla wrap
(approx 20 cm/8 in diameter)
1 egg
15 g (½ oz) butter
¼ red onion, finely chopped
¼ red pepper, diced
leaves from one sprig of thyme
pinch paprika
1 tomato, deseeded and diced
2–3 drops Tabasco sauce (optional)
25 g (1 oz) Cheddar cheese, grated
1 tbsp soured cream to serve
(optional)
salt and pepper

◉ Put the tortilla wrap on a large plate. Beat the egg with 1 teaspoon of water and a little salt and pepper.

◉ Heat half of the butter in a 20 cm (8 in) non-stick frying pan. Add the egg and tip the pan to spread out and make a thin omelette. Cook for 2–3 minutes, until the omelette has set, then slide it onto the tortilla.

◉ Heat the remaining butter in the frying pan and when foaming, add the onion, red pepper, thyme and paprika and sauté for 5 minutes, until the onion and pepper are soft. Add the tomato and cook for another 2 minutes, until the tomato is soft.

◉ Add the Tabasco sauce (if using) and season. Take the pan off the heat and set aside for a moment.

◉ Heat the tortilla and omelette for 10–20 seconds in a microwave, spoon the pepper and onion mixture over the centre, sprinkle over the cheese and roll up. Serve immediately with a spoonful of soured cream, if you like.

◉ If you prefer you can cut the omelette into little strips and mix in with the onion and red pepper mixture.

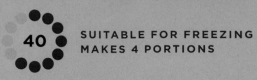
Tomato soup

Here are some tasty, simple-to-prepare soups

2 tsp olive oil
1 large celery stick, thinly sliced
1 large onion, finely chopped
1 carrot, peeled and grated
    (80 g/3 oz)
1 garlic clove, crushed
400 g (14 oz) tin chopped tomatoes
300 ml (½ pint) vegetable or
    chicken stock
2 large ripe tomatoes, quartered
1 tsp tomato purée
¼ tsp brown sugar (optional)

◉ Heat the oil in a saucepan. Add the celery, onion, carrot and garlic and fry for 5 minutes.

◉ Add the remaining ingredients. Bring to the boil, then simmer for 10–15 minutes, covered with a lid until all the vegetables are soft.

◉ Blend until smooth using a hand blender.

Lentil and vegetable soup

Lentils are a good source of protein and iron. A good way to get children to enjoy eating them is to whiz them up with sautéed vegetables to make a delicious soup.

2 tsp olive oil
1 onion, finely chopped
1 carrot, peeled and grated
   (80g/3 oz)
1 clove garlic, crushed
2 sticks celery, thinly sliced
50 g (2 oz) red lentils
200 g (7 oz) tin chopped tomatoes
600 ml (1 pint) vegetable stock
1 tsp sundried tomato paste
½ tsp brown sugar (optional)

◉ Heat the oil in a saucepan. Add the vegetables and fry for 2–3 minutes.

◉ Add the dried lentils and coat in the vegetable mixture. Then add the remaining ingredients.

◉ Bring to the boil, then simmer covered with a lid for 20–25 minutes, until the vegetables and lentils are soft.

◉ Whiz until smooth, using a hand blender.

Sweet potato and butternut squash soup with cheesy croutons

This flavoursome soup is enough on its own, but served with cheesy croutons is a real treat.

2 tbsp olive oil
1 small onion, chopped
½ tsp ginger, grated
200 g (7 oz) butternut squash, peeled and diced
150 g (5½ oz) sweet potato, peeled and diced
450 ml (15 fl oz) chicken stock

For the croutons
2 slices white bread
a little olive oil
2 tbsp Parmesan cheese, finely grated

◉ Heat the oil in a saucepan. Add the onion and ginger and fry for 3 minutes. Add the diced potato and squash.

◉ Fry for 2 minutes, then add the stock. Bring to the boil, then simmer for 15 minutes. Whiz using a hand blender, until smooth.

◉ To make the croutons, stamp 4 stars out of the white bread using a star cutter. Lightly brush with a little oil and sprinkle with the cheese.

◉ Put the croutons onto a baking sheet. Grill for 2–3 minutes, until lightly golden. Serve on top of the soup.

Rainbow ribbon noodles

It's fun eating these with child-friendly chopsticks that are joined at the top.

For the omelette
1 tbsp sunflower oil
1 egg
1 tsp soy sauce

For the noodles
1 tsp water
small clove garlic, crushed
½ tsp fresh ginger, grated
1 small carrot, peeled and cut into
    matchsticks
¼ yellow pepper, deseeded and
    cut into matchsticks
½ skinny courgette, cut into
    matchsticks
75 g (3 oz) medium rice noodles
    (pad Thai type) prepared
    according to the packet
    instructions or 150 g (5½ oz)
    fresh noodles
2 spring onions, thinly sliced
2 tsp soy sauce
1 tsp sweet chilli sauce
½ tsp sesame oil
fresh coriander, chopped (optional)

◉ Heat 1 teaspoon of the oil in a wok. Beat the egg, 1 teaspoon soy sauce and water together and add to the wok.

◉ Cook the egg until just set and brown underneath. Break or chop into pieces and transfer to a bowl. Set aside.

◉ Heat the remaining oil in the wok and add garlic and ginger. Sizzle for 30 seconds, then add the carrot, pepper and courgette and stir-fry for 3–4 minutes, until the vegetables are tender.

◉ Add the noodles and spring onions and stir-fry for 1–2 minutes, until the noodles have heated through. Stir in the soy sauce, sweet chilli sauce and sesame oil, followed by the omelette pieces, then remove from the heat and transfer to bowls.

◉ Garnish with chopped coriander, if you like.

Double-quick desserts and sweet treats

Strawberry and watermelon ice lollies

15

A refreshing treat during the watermelon season.

MAKES 6 SMALL ICE LOLLIES
50 g (2 oz) caster sugar
60 ml (2½ fl oz) water
250 g (9 oz) strawberries
250 g (9 oz) watermelon, cubed and deseeded

◉ Put the sugar and water into a small saucepan and boil until syrupy (about 3 minutes). Allow to cool. Purée the strawberries and sieve to get rid of the seeds.

◉ Purée the watermelon and mix with the puréed strawberries and cooled syrup. Pour the mixture into ice-lolly moulds and freeze.

lychee ice lollies

5

A delicious mix of lychees blended with vanilla yoghurt.

MAKES 3 ICE LOLLIES
425g (15 oz) tin lychees in syrup, drained
2 tbsp syrup from the tin
4 tbsp whole milk vanilla yogurt
1 tbsp lime juice

◉ Whiz the ingredients together, until fairly smooth. Pour into ice-lolly moulds and freeze overnight.

Strawberry and elderflower lolly

5

The elderflower adds a nice zesty taste to these lollies.

MAKES 4 LARGE LOLLIES
225 g (8 oz) strawberries, hulled
3 tbsp elderflower cordial
2 tbsp icing sugar

◉ Purée the strawberries, elderflower cordial and icing sugar and sieve.

◉ Pour into ice-lolly moulds.

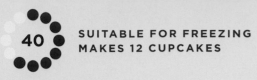

lemon cupcakes

Children love to help pipe the icing on cupcakes, so get them involved!

110g unsalted butter at room
   temperature
200g caster sugar
2 large eggs
150g self raising flour, sifted
125g plain flour, sifted
Half tsp baking powder
150 ml semi skimmed milk
1 tsp grated lemon zest

Frosting
200g icing sugar
80g unsalted butter at room
   temperature
1 tbsp lemon juice
2 tbsp cream cheese

◉ Preheat the oven to 180°C /Fan 160°C/350°F. Line a muffin tin with 12 paper cupcake cases.

◉ To make the cupcakes, measure all of the cake ingredients into a bowl. Whisk together until smooth.

◉ Spoon the mixture into the cupcake cases until two thirds full. Bake in the oven for about 25 minutes until they are raised and lightly golden. To check they are cooked you can insert a skewer or toothpick into the centre of one of the cakes and it should come out clean. Remove from the oven allow to cool down a little and then arrange the cupcakes on a wire rack to cool down completely.

◉ To make the frosting, sift the icing sugar and gradually beat it into the butter using an electric mixer until smooth. Slowly beat in the lemon juice and cream cheese at the end. Chill until needed. Spread the icing on top of the cup cake using a spatula or pipe the icing on top of each of the cupcakes.

Fruit compote

You can serve this either as breakfast or a dessert.

3 sweet eating apples
50 g (2 oz) sugar, plus extra to taste
450 g (1 lb) package frozen,
**   mixed berries**

◉ Peel and quarter the apples and cut each quarter into 4 pieces. Put the apples in a large saucepan with 2 tablespoons of water and the sugar.

◉ Heat gently, stirring occasionally until the sugar has melted. Cover and cook 8 minutes, until the apple is tender but not mushy.

◉ Add the frozen fruit and cook for a further 5–6 minutes, until the mixture just comes to a boil. Immediately remove from the heat and leave to cool slightly.

◉ Taste and add more sugar if necessary. Serve warm or chilled

Variations

◉ Once chilled the compote can be layered in glasses with yoghurt and granola or put in heatproof dishes.

◉ Whip 100 ml (3½ fl oz) double cream with 1 teaspoon icing sugar and 2–3 drops vanilla. Fold through 3 tablespoons Greek yoghurt and spoon over the fruit. Sprinkle 1 tablespoon demerara sugar over each and grill until the sugar has melted. You will need to drain away most of the liquid in the fruit and you could serve this separately in a jug.

Frozen berry smoothie

5

You can either buy a bag of frozen berry fruits or freeze some fresh berries overnight.

MAKES 2 GLASSES
150 g (5½ oz) frozen berries (raspberries, blackberries, blackcurrants or strawberries)
1 small banana
4 tbsp strawberry drinking yoghurt
100 ml (3½ fl oz) cream soda

◉ Put the frozen berries and banana into a food processor and whiz together until smooth. Pass through a sieve into a bowl. Add the yoghurt and cream soda and stir together. Pour into chilled glasses and serve.

Strawberry and banana smoothie

5

Choose a ripe banana and sweet strawberries for this smoothie. Personally I prefer to use a cloudy apple juice.

MAKES 2 GLASSES
1 large banana
150 g (5½ oz) strawberries
100 ml (3½ fl oz) apple juice

◉ Put all the ingredients into a food processor and whiz until smooth. Pour into 2 tumblers. Add ice cubes.

Strawberry sorbet ●● 10

If you don't have an ice-cream maker, freeze in a plastic carton and soften and whiz a couple of times in a food processor until frozen.

MAKES 4 PORTIONS
400 g (14 oz) strawberries, hulled and sliced
100 ml (3½ fl oz) water
100 g (3½ oz) strawberry or raspberry jam
100 g (3½ oz) sugar
4 tbsp Greek yoghurt

◉ Put the strawberries, water, jam and sugar in a saucepan. Heat gently until the sugar has melted, then bring to the boil and par-boil for 1 minute.

◉ Remove from the heat, cool, blend and sieve to remove seeds. Stir in the yoghurt and chill.

◉ Churn in an ice cream maker until frozen.

Banana bread ● 60

This is delicious for breakfast or as a snack. It's best made with very ripe bananas. It's lovely and moist, and keeps very well.

SUITABLE FOR FREEZING
MAKES 8 PORTIONS
450 g (1 lb) ripe bananas, peeled
110 g (4 oz) soft butter
120 g (4½ oz) soft light-brown sugar
225 g (8 oz) self-raising flour
1 egg
4 tbsp low fat yoghurt
1 tsp vanilla extract
125 g (4½ oz) raisins

◉ Preheat the oven to 180°C/350°F/Gas 4.

◉ Line a 900 g (2 lb) loaf tin with baking parchment.

◉ Put the bananas in a food processor and whiz for about 30 seconds, until roughly chopped. Add all other ingredients, except the raisins, and whiz for 1–2 minutes, until combined into a smooth batter. Add the raisins.

◉ Spoon into the loaf tin. Bake for 1 hour, until a skewer inserted into the centre comes out clean. Cool in the tin for 30 minutes, then remove the loaf from the tin and cool completely on a wire rack.

Crumble jumble

When babies first move from purées to soft foods it is useful to have some flavours that are familiar, such as blueberries, apples and pears. The fruit in crumbles is soft enough to be munched by gums, but not so soft that it is a purée. Older children and grown-ups also love crumbles. Here I have given you 3 different toppings and 3 different fillings, which you can mix and match as you like – there are 9 possible combinations! The quantities are for a large crumble baked in a 20 cm (8 in) diameter round baking dish (about 1.5 litre/2½ pints capacity) or 6 ramekins (200 ml/7 fl oz capacity).

● ● ● ● ● ● ● ● ● ● ● ● ●
TIP
If you are making a crumble topping, try making a double quantity and freezing half in a resealable bag. You can sprinkle the topping directly over the fruit base.

TOPPINGS
Classic crumble

85 g (3 oz) flour
45 g (1¾ oz) butter, cut into cubes
45 g (1¾ oz) demerara sugar
¾ tsp cinnamon
¼ tsp salt

Ginger oat

75 g (3 oz) plain flour
25 g (1 oz) rolled oats
50 g (2 oz) butter
½ tsp ground ginger
Pinch salt
45 g (1¾ oz) soft, light brown sugar

Flaky almond

75 g (3 oz) plain flour
25 g (1 oz) flaked almonds, plus an extra
   25 g (1 oz) for optional topping
45 g (1¾ oz) cold butter
45 g (1¾ oz) golden caster sugar
¼ tsp ground cinnamon

Whiz ingredients in a food processor until it forms large crumbs and looks like rolled oats. Sprinkle over the fruit.

Optional Scatter the extra 25 g (1 oz) flaked almonds over the crumble for the last 10 minutes of the cooking time.

Rhubarb and apple

2 large Granny Smith apples (400 g/14 oz)
   peeled, cored and diced
300 g (10½ oz) rhubarb, trimmed and cut into
   1 cm (3/8 in) lengths
100 g (3½ oz) caster sugar

◉ Toss the apples, rhubarb and sugar together in the dish. Sprinkle over your chosen topping and bake in an oven preheated to 200°C/400°F/Gas 6 for 35–40 minutes, until the topping is tinged with brown and the juices of the fruit are bubbling. For individual crumbles bake for 25–30 minutes.

Apple and blueberry

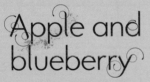

300 g (10½ oz) blueberries
2 large granny Smith apples (about 400 g/14 oz),
   peeled, cored and diced
Zest of one lemon (optional)
55 g (2 oz) sugar

◉ Toss the blueberries, apples, lemon zest (if using) and sugar together in the dish. Sprinkle over your chosen topping and bake in an oven preheated to 200°C/400°F/Gas 6 for 35–40 minutes, until the topping is tinged with brown and the juices of the fruit are bubbling. For individual crumbles bake for 25–30 minutes.

Orchard fruits

2 eating apples, peeled, cored and diced
2 large pears, peeled, cored and diced
4 tsp granulated sugar (or to taste)

◉ Put the fruit in a small saucepan and cook gently for 10–15 minutes, until it is soft but not mushy.

◉ Remove the fruit from the heat and stir in the granulated sugar, adding more if the fruit isn't sweet enough.

◉ Transfer to the baking dish, sprinkle over your chosen topping and bake in an oven preheated to 200°C/400°F/Gas 6 for 30 minutes, until the topping is tinged with brown. For individual crumbles bake for 25 minutes.

Annabel's oat bars

40

NOT SUITABLE FOR FREEZING
MAKES 12 BARS
85 g (3 oz) butter
90 g (3 oz) brown sugar
55 g (2 oz) golden syrup
100 g (3½ oz) oats
30 g (1 oz) Rice Krispies
¼ tsp salt
40 g (1½ oz) desiccated coconut
40 g (1½ oz) chopped dried apricots (ready to eat)
30 g (1oz) cranberries
30 g (1oz) raisins
40 g (1½ oz) chopped pecans (optional)

◉ Preheat the oven to 170°C/325° F/Gas 3.

◉ Line a 20 cm (8 in) square tin with baking parchment, with the parchment coming up the sides.

◉ Put the butter, sugar and golden syrup in a large saucepan.

◉ Heat gently, stirring occasionally, until butter and sugar have melted. Remove from the heat and mix in the remaining ingredients. Spoon into the prepared tin and press out in an even layer (a potato masher is useful). Bake for 25 minutes, until golden around the edges. Cool completely in the tin, then lift out and cut into 12 small bars. You may need to store these in the fridge.

Chocolate and apricot Rice Krispie squares

15

NOT SUITABLE FOR FREEZING
MAKES 9 SQUARES
75 g (3 oz) unsalted butter
75 g (3 oz) golden syrup
60 g (2½ oz) plain chocolate, broken into pieces
60 g (2½ oz) rolled oats
60 g (2½ oz) Rice Krispies
60 g (2½ oz) chopped dried apricots or mixture of dried exotic fruits

◉ Put the butter, golden syrup and chocolate into a medium saucepan and heat gently until melted.

◉ Combine the oats, Rice Krispies and chopped dried apricots in a mixing bowl.

◉ Remove from the heat. Pour the dry ingredients into the melted chocolate mixture and stir until well coated.

◉ Press the mixture into a 20 cm (8 in) square shallow baking tin and store in the fridge. Cut into squares and keep them there until ready to serve.

Chocolate courgette muffins 40

SUITABLE FOR FREEZING
MAKES 10 LARGE OR 24 MINI MUFFINS
175 g (6 oz) plain flour
2 tsp baking powder
150 g (5½ oz) soft-brown sugar
25 g (1 oz) cocoa powder
125 g (4½ oz) courgette, grated
   zest of 1 small orange (grated)
120 ml (4 fl oz) sunflower oil
1 egg, beaten
4 tbsp Greek yogurt or natural yogurt (not low fat)
1 tsp vanilla extract
50 g (2 oz) milk chocolate chips

◉ Preheat the oven to 180°C/350°F/Gas 4.

◉ Put the flour, baking powder, sugar, cocoa, courgette and orange zest into a mixing bowl.

◉ Put the oil, egg, yogurt and vanilla into a jug.

◉ Add the wet ingredients to the dry and mix together until smooth. Stir in the chocolate chips. Divide the mixture into 10 large muffin cases or 24 mini muffin cases. Bake the small muffins for about 14 minutes and the large muffins for 20–25 minutes, until the muffins are well risen and springy to the touch. Cool on a wire rack.

Carrot, apple and sultana muffins 35

SUITABLE FOR FREEZING
MAKES 12 MUFFINS
200 g (7 oz) self-raising flour
1 tsp baking powder
3/4 tsp bicarbonate of soda
1½ tsp mixed spice
½ tsp ginger
200 ml (7 fl oz) sunflower oil
100 g (3½ oz) caster sugar
2 eggs
100 g (3½ oz) carrots, grated
100 g (3½ oz) apple, peeled and grated
75 g (3 oz) sultanas

◉ Preheat the oven to 180°C/350° F/Gas 4.

◉ Put all the ingredients into a bowl. Whisk together using an electric hand whisk, until blended. Spoon into 12 deep bun/muffin tins lined with deep paper cases.

◉ Bake for 18–20 minutes until golden and well risen.

Chocolate self-saucing pudding

⚫ 55

MAKES 6 PORTIONS

For the chocolate sponge
50 g (2 oz) soft butter, plus extra for greasing
50 g (2 oz) soft light-brown sugar
100 g (3½ oz) self-raising flour
30 g (1 oz) cocoa powder
90 ml (3 fl oz) milk
1 egg
½ tsp vanilla extract
pinch salt
30 g (1 oz) chocolate chips

For the sauce
100 g (3½ oz) soft light-brown sugar
2 tbsp cocoa powder
1 tsp instant coffee granules
200 ml (7 fl oz) boiling water

⚫ Preheat the oven to 170°C/ 325°F/Gas 3. Grease a 1.5 litre (2½ pint) deep baking dish. Put all the sponge ingredients, except the chocolate chips, in a food processor and whiz for 1–2 minutes to combine. Add the chocolate chips and pulse 4–5 times to distribute. Scrape the batter into the prepared dish.

⚫ Whisk the sauce ingredients together in a heatproof bowl or jug and pour over the sponge batter. Bake for 35–40 minutes, until the sponge has risen and a skewer inserted into the centre comes out without any raw batter on it. The sauce will also be bubbling up the sides of the sponge. Serve with vanilla ice cream

Creamy chocolate pots

⚫ 25

MAKES 4 SMALL POTS
300 ml (½ pint) milk (not low fat)
60 ml (2 fl oz) double cream
2 egg yolks
4 tsp cornflour
75 g (3 oz) caster sugar
50 g (2 oz) chopped dark chocolate
½ tsp vanilla extract
small knob (about 5 g/1 tsp) butter

⚫ Put the milk and cream in a saucepan. Heat gently until almost boiling. Meanwhile put egg yolks, cornflour and sugar in a bowl and whisk together.

⚫ Pour the hot milk and cream onto the egg mixture in a thin stream, whisking constantly. Rinse the saucepan to remove any milk on the base. Then pour the custard into the pan and cook over medium-low heat, whisking or stirring constantly, until the custard just comes up to the boil and thickens. Remove from the heat and whisk in the chocolate, vanilla and butter.

⚫ Pour into 4 small ramekins and chill 5–6 hours (or overnight) until set. You can press a piece of clingfilm onto the surface of each chocolate cup if you want to prevent a skin forming.

Index

Annabel Karmel is the UK's best-selling author on baby and children's food and nutrition. She is an expert in devising tasty and nutritious meals for children without the need for parents to spend hours in the kitchen.

A mother of three, Annabel is the best-selling cookery writer on feeding children. She has written 22 books including *Complete Baby and Toddler Meal Planner*, *Complete Family Meal Planner*, *The Fussy Eaters Recipe Book* and *Top 100 Pasta Dishes*. Her books have sold over 4 million copies worldwide. Her Complete Baby and Toddler Meal Planner has become the authoritative guide on feeding babies and children and is regularly in the top five cookery titles.

Books are not the only string to Annabel's bow; she has created the Eat Fussy range of chilled meals, which is now the number-one range of branded ready meals for children in supermarkets. She has the popular Make it Easy range of equipment for preparing baby food. Annabel has also created a co-branded range of Healthy Foods for young children with Disney, and has developed her own collection of cooking equipment for aspiring junior chefs.

Annabel is passionate about improving the way children eat in popular family attractions, hotels, pubs and restaurants, and her menus can be found in all the major theme parks including Legoland and Thorpe Park, as well the UK's largest Holiday Park group – Haven Holidays and Butlins. In 2009 Annabel won a prestigious Caterer and Hotelkeeper Excellence in Food award for her children's meals, as well as the Lifetime Achievement award at the Mother and Baby Awards in 2009.

Her popular website www.annabelkarmel.com has more than 80,000 members, and offers parents delicious recipes for babies, children and adults, as well as information on all aspects of nutrition.

Annabel has recently launched her own TV series, *Annabel's Kitchen*, an entertainment series on CiTV and ITV1. The series is no ordinary children's cookery show. It features a magical array of penguin puppets and wacky inventions to help the children with their cooking dilemmas and encourage them to try out new recipes. Based in Annabel's loft apartment, Annabel and her two assistants, Jimmy and Pearl the penguins, help the children with their cooking and have some fun and often hilarious adventures doing so.

Annabel was awarded an MBE in June 2006 in the Queen's Birthday Honours for her outstanding work in the field of child nutrition.

www.annabelkarmel.com

ACKNOWLEDGEMENTS

I would like to thank the following for their help and work on this book: Dave King for his excellent photography; Smith & Gilmour for their beautiful design; Liz Thomas for hair and make-up: food stylist Seiko Hatfield; Lucinda Kaicik; Jo Harris for her props styling; the team at Ebury Press, including Fiona Macintyre, Carey Smith and Hannah Knowles; and Helena Caldon and Jo Godfrey Wood. A big thank you to all the lovely children who were involved in the photoshoot: Alfie, Charlie, Dexter, Katie, Lily, Leah, Lucas, Oscar and Poppy and Sophie.

Lastly but by no means least, I would like to thank my children, Nicholas, Lara and Scarlett, for tasting all my recipes.

Get recipes at your fingertips!

Download Annabel's iPhone App, *Annabel's Essential Guide to Feeding Your Baby & Toddler*, and get 100 nutritious recipes for babies, toddlers and the whole family plus cooking videos, advice & top tips. **Available from the App store.**

An easy option for busy mums!

With Annabel Karmel's chilled meals in your fridge, you will always have a tasty and nutritious dish for your growing toddler, even when you don't have time to prepare something yourself. **Available from major supermarkets.**